To Dan,

With much RESPECT and appreciation. It has been a pleasure working with you and your team.

Best,

P.s. Continue to be a great leader who is never hesitant to have those critical conversations!

"This book provides crystal clear advice on how to turn difficult conversations into productive ones. In *Let's Talk About It*, Dr. Marciano has distilled his 30 years of transforming workplace relationships into universal, easy-to-implement strategies that we can all use to improve important relationships in our professional and personal lives."

—ELIOT BRENNER, PhD, Executive Director
of Klingenstein Philanthropies

"*Let's Talk About It* should be required reading, regardless of what position or industry you are in. This is an easy read with effective tips to make anyone, at any level, a better communicator. Successful leaders communicate authentically and honestly. This book will help you become that leader."

—SHARON NOBLE, Vice President of Human
Resources at Huber Engineered Materials

"Having healthy conversations is the key to effective leadership and, ultimately, to organizational success. In *Let's Talk About It*, Dr. Marciano provides the communication strategy and tactics to achieve those twin goals."

—CHRISTOPHER J. PHELAN, President and CEO
of Hunterdon County Chamber of Commerce

"Marciano reminds us that creating inclusive and welcoming workplaces requires intentional and meaningful work—work that starts with the 'I' in *inclusion*. This work is not so much a destination as it is a journey of self-reflection, soul-searching, and commitment that will inevitably have communal impact. *Let's Talk About It* cultivates the common good by focusing on the *we*."

—CAROL E. HENDERSON, PhD, Vice Provost for
Diversity and Inclusion, Chief Diversity Officer, and
Adviser to the President of Emory University

"*Let's Talk About It* is an essential handbook that enables us to recognize how our biases, blind spots, and body language inform the manner in which we communicate. In today's fast-paced digital world, the book's scripts, scenarios, and best practices—especially in videoconferencing—will empower you to handle any communication conflict with confidence. Packed with solutions, it will equip you to foster and maintain healthy, respectful relationships."

—DIANE PIRAINO-KOURY, McDonald's
franchise owner and operator

"Relationships deepen because of, not in spite of, conflict. Dr. Marciano helps us transform conflict into opportunity, providing the tools (and courage) to convert negative emotion into successful conversations that produce positive outcomes."

—MELANIE KATZMAN, PhD, business
psychologist and #1 *Wall Street Journal*
bestselling author of *Connect First*

"Now more than ever, the skills we need to bridge divides, find common ground, and come together in joint purpose are even more critical to our success. If relationships are the foundation of that success, conversations are the glue. *Let's Talk About It* equips us with the necessary tools to build that strong foundation."

—JEREMEY DONOVAN, Senior Vice President
of Sales Strategy at SalesLoft and bestselling
author of *How to Deliver a TED Talk*

LET'S TALK ABOUT IT

LET'S TALK ABOUT IT

Turning Confrontation into
Collaboration at Work

PAUL L. MARCIANO, PHD

New York Chicago San Francisco Athens London Madrid
Mexico City Milan New Delhi Singapore Sydney Toronto

1 2 3 4 5 6 7 8 9   LCR   26 25 24 23 22 21

ISBN   978-1-260-47338-4
MHID   1-260-47338-4

e-ISBN 978-1-260-47339-1
e-MHID   1-260-47339-2

Library of Congress Cataloging-in-Publication Data

Names: Marciano, Paul L., author.
Title: Let's talk about it : turning confrontation into collaboration at work /
    Paul L. Marciano, PhD.
Description: New York : McGraw Hill, [2020] | Includes bibliographical
    references and index.
Identifiers: LCCN 2020043598 (print) | LCCN 2020043599 (ebook) |
    ISBN 9781260473384 (hardback) | ISBN 9781260473391 (ebook)
Subjects: LCSH: Conflict management. | Interpersonal conflict. |
    Interpersonal communication. | Communication in organizations. |
    Personnel management.
Classification: LCC HD42 .M376 2020 (print) | LCC HD42 (ebook) |
    DDC 658.3/145—dc23
LC record available at https://lccn.loc.gov/2020043598
LC ebook record available at https://lccn.loc.gov/2020043599

McGraw Hill books are available at special quantity discounts to use as premiums and sales promotions or for use in corporate training programs. To contact a representative, please visit the Contact Us pages at www.mhprofessional.com.

Jack, my best friend, I miss you every day

and

Kristen, my puzzle piece, I love you more each day

CONTENTS

ACKNOWLEDGMENTS

Throughout this project, my godchild, Amanda Eliades Zalla, has been a godsend. Her tangible and intangible contributions have been indispensable in bringing this book to life.

I am deeply grateful to the many organizations and leaders with whom I have worked, but none more so than Rob, TJ, and Michael Earle. Remaining faithful to their father's core values of quality, efficiency, and integrity, they have built Earle into an extraordinary company. It has been a privilege and an honor to be part of their journey.

I would like to acknowledge the following individuals for whom I have great respect and appreciation: Dr. Eliot Brenner at Klingenstein Philanthropies; Doug "Film Doc" Clayton at SES; Dr. Jim Dlugos at Saint Joseph's College of Maine; John Emmons at Mannington Mills; Dr. Carol Henderson at Emory University; Bill Hills at Navy Federal Credit Union; Dr. Alan Kazdin at Yale University; Kevin Kruse at LeadX; Chris Phelan at the Hunterdon Chamber of Commerce; Leah Pontani at Goodwill; Lily Prost, Daniel Krawczyk, and Sharon Noble at Huber; Dan Rehal at Vision2Voice Healthcare Communications; Sharon Werner at Marsh & McLennan Agency; and Dawn Wilno at Core Association Partners.

My thanks to those who shared their insights and stories from their "playing field," including Kristen Avery, Josh Budde, Michael Caldwell, Dr. David Desteno, Giles Garrison, Nancee Gelineau, John Hellier, Diane Koury, Robin Lapidus, Jean Larkin, Axel Larsson, Jack Licata, Sharon Mahn, Jeff Masters, Crista McNish, Erica Moffett, John

Parks, Krishnan Ramaswami, Laura Reilly, John Rice, Amanda Seirup, Kriste Jordan Smith, Warren Spitzer, Robert Stanisch, Timothy Theiss, and Joe Wingert.

I am so very grateful for the unconditional support of Jeanne Murphy and Colleen Kelly of Mariah Media, who, next to my mother, have been my greatest cheerleaders. Writing a book can be stressful at times (or all the time), and everyone needs a friend who can talk him off the ledge. My thanks to John Bradshaw for always being there and letting me talk about it. With love to Maddie, Taylor, Brady, and Katie whose lives give mine meaning. Finally, a nod to my friends at Beehive Poker League, who have proven over and over again that I am terrible at reading body language.

With gratitude.

—PLM

INTRODUCTION

I hate conflict; I really do. However, I have come to realize that avoiding it does not serve me or anyone else well. When I choose to bite my tongue and stop myself from discussing an issue that concerns or upsets me, I invariably become frustrated and then resentful not just toward the other person, but also toward myself for being too much of a wimp to initiate a conversation. Instead, I usually end up complaining to others in hopes of gaining sympathy under the guise of garnering advice. Sometimes I let my anger build to the point of losing my cool, and I speak sharply to the other person, which, frankly, is terribly unfair, as she may have had no idea that I was even upset. After losing my temper, I end up feeling worse about the situation because I have now demonstrated to myself and others that I cannot control my emotions, let alone deal with the problem effectively. Ironically, when we have problems in our relationships, we often avoid talking about them, and in the process make things worse.

Over my 30-plus year career, I have seen a lot of conflict in the workplace and the damage it does to relationships, morale, and productivity when it goes unaddressed. Among the more egregious examples that still make me shake my head include the manager who refused to speak to his direct report for two years, an employee who was fired over text because his manager wanted to avoid conflict, and two colleagues who did not speak for four months because one failed to copy the other on an email. Obviously, most situations are more mundane and subtle; I bet that a few examples have already come to your mind. Can you imagine the total number of interpersonal conflict situations that exist in the workplace at any one time and the adverse impact they have on individuals and organizations? Just think about how distracting these conflicts are and how much time and energy they take to both address and avoid.

I have come to believe that much conflict in the workplace (and the world) could be resolved or prevented altogether if people were skilled at straightforward conversations. Have you ever avoided having a difficult conversation, the simple thought of which caused your blood pressure to rise and heart to race? Have you ever regretted not having a critical conversation sooner because, in the end, not doing so made the situation worse? Have you gotten frustrated with yourself for not having the courage to address a person or situation head-on? Can you imagine how your life might change for the better if you could deal directly and effectively with any conflict in your life? If you answered "Yes" to any of these questions, then you did yourself a favor by picking up this book.

Difficult Conversations

A difficult conversation is one we believe will evoke strong negative emotions and likely involve conflict. In our minds, the conversation may become unpredictable and unsafe as tensions rise. Or, we might find the topic of the discussion embarrassing, making us vulnerable in some way. We might have to deliver bad or disappointing news. Or we may simply want to ask a question to which we fear the answer will be "No." In general, difficult conversations are those we anticipate will make us feel uncomfortable and may lead to a poor outcome. Examples of such situations include:

- ► Confronting a colleague who has taken credit for your work

- ► Discussing with a boss why you have been passed over for a promotion

- ► Furloughing or firing an employee

▶ Quitting

▶ Telling a coworker that he has bad breath or body odor

▶ Informing your supervisor about a costly mistake

▶ Notifying a customer that you cannot deliver what was promised

It is critical to realize that difficult conversations are difficult because we think they are. Conversations are not inherently good or bad, easy or difficult. They are so because we label them as such. If we say that something is "hard," then it is hard. Our thoughts and words shape our reality; moreover, we believe that we are never wrong. The assignment you were given is unfair because you say it was unfair. Your boss is a jerk because you say she is a jerk. Your colleague is conniving because you say he is conniving. How we choose to label people and situations makes them that way.

The extent to which we view situations as potentially easy or difficult depends largely on how competent we feel in taking them on. For example, I will not drive in New York City because I believe it to be far too difficult and stressful. I do not feel competent in my driving skills to navigate the stop-and-go traffic. (I am also embarrassed to say that I never learned to parallel park.) On the other hand, I do not find public speaking hard, which some people fear more than death. *In general, we experience stress whenever perceived environmental demands exceed our perceived internal resources.* Thus, most people avoid engaging in what they believe would be a difficult conversation because the thought of doing so causes anxiety. But what if we changed our mindset from telling ourselves we must face a difficult conversation to believing we have the skills to engage in a healthy conversation?

Healthy Conversations

I find that highly successful people are very good at dealing with conflict. They address interpersonal problems quickly in a straightforward, calm, and respectful manner. There is no finger-pointing or drama, and the goal is not to make the other person feel bad or guilt him into apologizing. A productive conversation takes place in which both people speak and listen to one another. The issue often gets resolved promptly, and importantly, both people leave the interaction feeling complete and move on without resentment. In short, they have learned how to have healthy conversations.

You will read a whole chapter on helpful mindsets, but for now I would like you to reframe difficult conversations into healthy conversations. Just as people who are good at giving corrective feedback think in terms of "constructive" rather than "critical," people who are good at dealing with conflict situations think of conversations in terms of "healthy" rather than "difficult." Approaching conversations in this way can help decrease the likelihood of defensiveness (on either side) and emotional escalation. Such conversations are more effective and efficient, which is advantageous for the relationship and for workplace productivity. What makes for such a conversation? Healthy conversations are characterized by the following:

- ► A two-way flow of communication in which both people have the opportunity to fully express their views, opinions, concerns, and feelings in a safe environment without fear of retribution or other negative impact.

- ► Both people feel heard and understood.

- ► Communication is transparent and straightforward; there is no distortion or withholding of information.

- ► The conversation remains respectful and professional.

- ► Each person remains calm and composed.

A healthy conversation does not mean that everyone gets exactly what they want. Being happy or even satisfied with the outcome is not part of the deal. For example, imagine your boss asks you to take on work unfinished by a colleague. You are not happy and ask to discuss it. The conversation might have all the elements of a healthy one, but, in the end, you still have to take on the responsibilities. It was a healthy conversation—it just did not go the way you wanted.

What to Expect

The goal of this book is to make you comfortable, confident, and competent in addressing and resolving conflict through healthy conversations. As with my previous title, *Carrots and Sticks Don't Work*, this book provides tangible and actionable strategies that will empower you to deal effectively with any workplace conflict. In this book you will learn about the unconscious cognitive biases that lead to systematic distortions in our thinking and how to deal with different personality types. You will discover the minefields and gold mines of language and learn specific communication strategies and techniques. Perhaps most importantly, you will find many anecdotes throughout the book and an entire appendix devoted to real-world scenarios and scripts to guide you through healthy conversations on your playing field. And while I certainly hope that you find this book an enjoyable and interesting read, my greatest hope is that it will make a difference in your life—both professionally and personally.

UP NEXT

In order to figure out how to address potentially difficult conversations, it is helpful to understand what triggers them in the first place. Let's find out.

ON YOUR PLAYING FIELD

1. Whom do you consider highly skilled in holding difficult conversations and resolving conflict? What does that person say and do that makes her so effective?
2. How would you evaluate yourself in terms of your willingness and ability to address and successfully resolve contentious issues?
3. Do you believe you can learn the skills necessary to have healthy conversations?

CHAPTER 1

ROOT CAUSES

When it comes to figuring out how best to deal with conflict, a good place to start is understanding the underlying issues and events that drive it. In fact, doing so may help us prevent problem situations from arising in the first place, rendering contentious conversations unnecessary. As you read over the following list of common causes of conflict in the workplace, think about how these situations were handled in your own experience and how they might have been dealt with differently:

- ► Perception of inequality in workload distribution; employees not pulling their weight and having their tasks consequently pushed onto other team members

- ► Perception of unfair or unequal pay; discord created by employees who perceive they are doing the same work as colleagues with equivalent credentials but for less pay

- ► Unfulfilled expectations: perceived broken promises, such as being led to expect a promotion or raise with no follow-through

- ► Poor communication: ambiguous, inaccurate, delayed, or a total lack of communication

► Ambiguous or unclear directions, instructions, or expectations

► Misaligned goals: for example, when the objectives of one department run counter to those of another, or when there is competition for resources

► Lack of clarity in job responsibilities: it is unclear who is responsible for what

► Decisions affecting individuals' work being made without their input

► When one's decisions, judgment, or character is questioned

► Public criticism; colleagues embarrassing one another

► Assigning blame, finger-pointing

► Constant negative or critical feedback

► Gossip; talking behind colleagues' backs

► Unfair treatment or work practices; showing favoritism, such as allowing certain employees greater flexibility in their work schedule than others

► Lack of recognition: when one does not receive due credit

► Poor performance: an employee being put on a performance improvement plan, formally reprimanded, or terminated

► Lack of accountability: an employee who has not been held accountable for poor performance

While not an exhaustive list, you can certainly see how common the causes of conflict are in the workplace—they occur every day! Just imagine how much time and energy are wasted worrying and gossiping about such issues. Imagine having the skills and confidence to address these situations and more.

SUMMARY

While the issues that elicit upset are varied, there is a common thread throughout: when people feel their "survival" in the workplace is threatened, they often become triggered. These root causes make people less able to do their jobs effectively, put them at a competitive disadvantage to coworkers, or in some way make them look bad. Any of these factors could limit the perceived value that employees bring to their organization, thus making them feel less relevant and expendable. They make people feel insecure.

UP NEXT

This book would not be necessary if people regularly addressed emotionally charged conversations in a straightforward manner. So why are most of us so resistant to doing so? In the next chapter we will review the many reasons that people choose to avoid difficult conversations.

ON YOUR PLAYING FIELD

1. Refer to the list of root causes and identify a few that have led you to experience workplace conflict.
2. Can you think of additional reasons that cause people to become upset?
3. Which issues do you think are the most difficult to address and why?
4. Are there any current conflicts you are refraining from addressing? (Throughout the book, you will want to return to this list and apply your learnings to resolve these situations.)

CHAPTER 2

I THINK I'LL PASS

When it comes to dealing with conflict, most of us would rather take a pass. We choose to avoid conflict whenever possible because it introduces risk and potential vulnerability. When it comes to our fight-or-flight instinct, flight often seems like the better choice—especially when "losing" is the likely outcome and has severe consequences, ergo getting fired. Thus, we often choose to keep our thoughts and concerns to ourselves—and we all probably remember times when we wish we had!

We are quite good at making excuses and rationalizing why avoiding conflict is the most sensible course of action. From a psychological perspective, coming up with sensible reasons for why we should not engage in a conversation serves us well because it reduces cognitive dissonance. (Cognitive dissonance is a theory proposed by Leon Festinger in which we seek to hold our cognitions—thoughts, opinions, beliefs—and behaviors in harmony with one another.) We naturally find mental discord unsettling and desire to bring our beliefs and actions into alignment. There are, of course, all kinds of problems associated with avoiding conflict—more on that in the next chapter. Right now, let's examine what we say to ourselves that allows us to "take a pass" on addressing situations with potential conflict. As you read, take note of your go-to excuses and consider the impact of *not* having such conversations.

5

"Having the Conversation Won't Make a Difference"

Have you ever felt that you have had the same conversation over and over, each instance leading to either short-lived change or no change at all? I know I have. This experience is so frustrating that at some point you simply declare to yourself, and oftentimes to others, that there is little point in revisiting the same topic yet again. And while giving up may seem the only sensible option, it leaves you feeling more frustrated and disempowered. If the same conversation has not led to the desired results, perhaps you should be having a different conversation—a healthy one.

"Having the Conversation Might Make Things Worse"

Often our fears of addressing a conversation extend past the worry that it will make no difference; we fear that addressing the problem will lead to an even bigger one. The potential upside to having the conversation is overshadowed by the potential downside. For example, a manager might avoid addressing the behavior of an underperforming employee for fear that he may quit, which would lead to increased work and stress for others, including the manager herself. On the other hand, when a manager fails to hold an employee accountable for fulfilling his job responsibilities, she often ends up unfairly punishing her best employees with additional work, who may end up becoming resentful and losing respect for their manager. (If a manager is afraid to address performance issues with a direct report, then she probably should not be a manager.)

"Having the Conversation Might Put Me in Jeopardy"

Some people are vindictive, and unfortunately, retaliation may be a real concern. When people sense that they are being called out or embarrassed in front of others, they may feel attacked and respond by going on the offensive. For example, the person could start spreading rumors throughout the workplace, sabotage another team member's work, or purposely provide misleading information. Of course, the riskiest situation may be confronting your manager regarding a concern you have about her behavior or, even riskier, taking your concerns to your manager's boss. To be clear, these may be valid concerns; at this point, however, just recognize that they are rationalizations for avoiding straight conversations.

"Time Will Make Things Better"

No, time will not make things better—in fact, it may make them worse. Unlike acne, interpersonal problems rarely clear up on their own. For example, imagine that two team members get into an argument and stop speaking. If time truly made the issue dissipate, their relationship would improve on its own. Typically, that is not what happens. People do not forget when they have been offended or disrespected. However, sometimes one or both parties will pretend as though nothing happened, which is both aggravating and unhealthy. I bet you can remember interactions that occurred many years ago that you never addressed and cause you angst to this day. Perhaps you are even thinking of one now. The double whammy is that in such situations you may end up being angry at yourself for not having spoken up. Talking with others about your concern or upset in a timely manner is not just helpful for getting things off your chest, it also increases the likelihood that you will have a healthy, calm conversation without accumulating weeks, months, or even years of resentment.

"Now Is Not a Good Time"

Sometimes we recognize that addressing an issue is necessary, but we justify holding off by telling ourselves that now is not a good time. (By the way, we use this excuse for all kinds of decisions and behaviors that we procrastinate in our lives, like writing a book.) We just have too much going on that needs our attention. This conversation can wait, especially if it means potentially "upsetting the apple cart" and causing us to expend time and energy that would distract us from our priorities. Sometimes we invoke empathy and tell ourselves that the timing is not good for the *other* person. For example, if a team member is clearly feeling overwhelmed, you might rationalize not wanting to cause him further stress. Ironically, he too may be avoiding the conversation, and your bringing it up would be a relief. Having a straightforward discussion in a timely manner helps ensure that things do not get swept under the rug and lead to ongoing animosity. The longer we wait, the less likely we are to address the situation and the more awkward it will feel when we do.

"The Situation Isn't at a Point Where It Really Needs to Be Addressed"

So should one just wait until the problem gets worse? This justification is used by managers the world over seeking to avoid discussing performance problems with employees, such as a team member who has been sporadically showing up late to meetings. Employees also use this excuse to avoid addressing problems with coworkers. For example, you may have a highly extroverted and social team member who keeps stopping by your desk to chat. It is annoying, but you do not want to hurt his feelings and so you just try to keep the conversations short. Unfortunately, he seems to be stopping by more frequently as time goes on. At what point is enough enough? It is far easier to address and extinguish problem behavior when it first arises than to let it escalate. Dealing with a small mess now is better than dealing with a big mess later!

"This Discussion Will Bring Up Other Issues That I Really Don't Want to Address"

Hopefully, it does. (You do see the irony in this rationalization, right?) Often, tense conversations do give rise to issues the other person has been refraining from discussing. Sometimes, when a conversation becomes too intense, a person will try to steer it to a less threatening topic. Should other issues surface, acknowledge and commit to addressing them but stay focused on the reason for the current discussion.

"I Might End Up Looking Like the Bad Guy"

Being liked is really important to most of us. Often, we rationalize that if we draw attention to certain issues we will be viewed in a negative light—jealous, petty, or whiny. For example, imagine working on a factory floor where assignments are supposed to be rotated among team members, but you always seem to get stuck doing the least desirable jobs. Or there are people on the team spending more time on social media than they are working. While you may have a strong desire to talk to your manager about such situations, you will likely refrain from doing so to avoid seeming like a complainer or tattletale. Instead, you end up biting your tongue and becoming resentful of your colleagues. Handling the situation using the techniques in this book will leave you looking like a responsible team member and eliminate any resentment.

"I Don't Want to Get My Friend in Trouble"

Sometimes we are put in a terrible position when a friend at work is doing something wrong or inappropriate and we know about it, especially if they ask us not to say anything. Imagine, for example, a colleague who begins to fudge her time sheet, claims to have checked over her work when you know she has not, or blames another team member when it was she who actually made the mistake. In such instances, you likely know that you should say something but cannot bring yourself to do so. You'd better hope that your friend does not really screw up and your manager does not find out you knew about the issue all along. As is the case in most things, honesty is the best policy, if not in the short term then definitely in the long term.

"We Have a Good Working Relationship, and I Don't Want to Risk Messing It Up"

I have successfully argued myself out of having all kinds of direct conversations in the name of preserving a relationship. I think to myself, "If I bring this up, it could really cause friction." Imagine having a colleague who does something that irritates you, and he's been doing so for quite a while. For example, he is always late to video-conferences, or he speaks loudly during phone calls, most of which are of a personal nature and last for long periods of time. Or, he constantly checks his social media accounts and then complains about having too much work and asks for help. If you do not address these issues, they will keep coming up. Eventually you will start taking your frustration out on your colleague in ways that will damage the relationship, which is precisely what you tried to avoid in the first place. As my friend and client Sharon Noble puts it, "If you don't talk about it, you'll act it out."

"I Don't Want to Hurt the Other Person's Feelings"

Most of us have probably had the experience of working with someone who dressed unprofessionally, had bad breath or body odor, put on too much cologne or perfume, or spoke too loudly. Or maybe someone was very proud of his work, which, quite frankly, was not all that good, but you did not want to burst his bubble. (Hopefully, my friends and family reading this book will continue to feign praise.) We really, really want to avoid having awkward conversations around such personal topics. I was once asked by a client to tell an employee that he stood too close when speaking. At first, the employee was terribly embarrassed. Then he was upset that in the four years he had worked for the company, no one had ever brought this issue up. In such situations, I always put myself in the other person's shoes and ask, "Would I want to know that?" Almost invariably the answer is "Yes." It is my firm belief that you can tell anyone almost anything if it comes from a place of caring and if you do so with some tact.

"I'm Waiting for the Other Person to Bring It Up"

Bad idea. There are many conversations I have never initiated because I got it in my head that the other person was at fault, and thus it was her responsibility to apologize to me. Meanwhile, the other person may be completely unaware there is even an issue in need of discussion. On the other hand, she could be waiting for you to bring it up. If you never have a discussion, you will never resolve the issue. Stop waiting and start talking about it.

"I Don't Really Care"

Yes, you do care, or you would not be having this conversation with yourself. We tell ourselves we do not care because we are afraid that addressing the issue will not go as we hope—for example, that the other person will not apologize or things will get worse. Telling yourself that you do not care and avoiding the conversation will not get rid of the pit in your stomach. Also, do not go down the path of "I'll be the bigger person" or play the martyr. You are going to resent yourself for lacking courage, and you will lose the respect of others who see that you are not willing to stand up for yourself.

"I Don't Know What to Say or How to Say It"

That is why I wrote this book. In coaching clients throughout my career, the most common reason people give for not having a critical conversation is that they do not know how. "Where do I begin?" I realized that people's lack of confidence is often authentically based on a lack of competence. Having a difficult conversation does not take courage; it takes skill. Fortunately, by the time you finish this book, you will have those skills and know exactly what to say and how to say it.

▶ ▶ ▶

Wow, we certainly have lots of conversations with ourselves so we can avoid having them with others! *You need to ask yourself whether you are more committed to avoiding conflict or to having a healthy relationship.* While the road of avoidance may seem like an easier one in the short term, the longer we stay on it, the rougher the terrain and the tougher it gets to effectively address the problem. In some cases, there is no turning back. Understand that when you choose not to address conflict, you are making a choice, one that will likely have an adverse impact on you, the other person, and/or your team.

SUMMARY

We allow ourselves to entertain so many reasons to avoid addressing conflict, some of which can be quite legitimate. However, regardless of how justified our reasoning, the result is the same: we choose not to address the problem and become resentful as a result, which leads to a further deterioration in the relationship. Instead of convincing yourself that it would be safer to forgo a conversation, you would be better off talking yourself into one.

UP NEXT

Choosing to avoid addressing critical issues may sound like a good idea, but it has serious consequences. In the next chapter, we will discuss the adverse impact of avoidance on ourselves and others.

ON YOUR PLAYING FIELD

1. Review the list of rationalizations and put a check mark next to those that you have used in the past. How many did you identify? Which excuses do you use most frequently?
2. Are there any other reasons than those listed that you use to let yourself off the hook?
3. Take a look back at the issues you identified in the previous chapter. What are you saying to yourself to put off the conversations? Do you see them now more as excuses than objective reasons?

CHAPTER 3

AVOIDANCE COSTS

voiding conflict has consequences, however, and these consequences are typically more problematic than the issues you are avoiding. Yes, there are circumstances under which dropping the matter makes sense, such as a minor conflict with a colleague or one that is not repeated when a team member's behavior was completely out of character, and you know that she was under tremendous stress. More likely, however, not addressing the problem will cause discord to exacerbate and resentment to fester. The fallout also often impacts others in the organization. In this chapter, we will discuss why letting ourselves off the hook can leave us *on* the hook for lots more conflict. As you read, reflect on your own experiences and the costs to you and others.

Individual-Level Impact

In general, avoiding a conversation with someone is exhausting and disempowering. Just think about the person in your life you dread having to walk past in the hallway. (Or that former friend you desperately hope did not see you turning down the grocery store aisle.) We expend a great deal of mental and emotional energy figuring out how to avoid people with whom we have developed a contentious relationship. At work, interpersonal conflict can lead to feelings of bitterness, anger, sadness, and frustration that spill over and impact our personal life. The longer we go without addressing the emotional thorn, the stronger and further entrenched our negative feelings become. This may, in fact, contribute to psychological and physical health problems. Have you ever felt a gnawing pit in your stomach because, ironically, you avoided a conversation you thought you could not stomach? I find that when I choose to initiate a conversation I have actively avoided, I invariably feel better about myself, regardless of the outcome. In some ways, I feel like a coward when I choose avoidance, and I feel courageous and powerful when I speak up. Saying what you have to say is often very liberating. Let's take a look at some examples.

In my experience, sadly, people would rather tolerate being miserable at work than take the initiative to discuss their concerns, especially if it involves their manager. Krishnan, a good friend, worked in an accounting firm and was a talented, trusted, and dedicated team member. Over time, his manager, Brady, came to rely on him more and more, which translated into more and more work. While he was a great employee who had enjoyed his job, Krishan became overwhelmed and frustrated. He also began feeling taken advantage of as his additional efforts and positive results were not accompanied by a promotion or a raise. The real rub, however, was that Brady rarely acknowledged or gave Krishnan credit for his accomplishments. In fact, Brady would often take the credit. Over the course of a year, Krishnan grew increasingly angry and resentful. One day, Brady asked him to take on yet another assignment far outside the scope of his core job responsibilities. It was Krishnan's tipping point. Much to Brady's surprise, Krishnan cleaned out his desk, dropped off his badge and laptop, and walked out.

During this period, I encouraged Krishnan to confront his manager and discuss the issue. Maybe Brady was overwhelmed himself and oblivious to his unfair treatment of Krishnan. He may have been insensitive but not intentionally taking advantage of Krishnan. After all, Krishnan had always stepped up and never complained, so why should Brady be concerned? Krishnan would just look at me, shake his head, and say that confronting his manager would make no difference. Maybe not, I would tell him, but one thing was for sure—the situation would not improve if he did not. If he was willing to quit anyway, what possible downside was there to having a straightforward conversation? Regardless of the outcome, I am certain that Krishnan would have felt better if he had stood up for himself.

This next example involves conflict between peers. Aisha and Taylor worked together in the finance department of a large manufacturing company. Taylor began spearheading teamwide Friday happy hours at a nearby microbrewery. However, he never asked Aisha to join. She began to feel ostracized, hurt, and confused about why she was not being included. Had she done something to offend Taylor, or was there someone else on the team who did not want her to be invited? After a few weeks, Aisha decided to confront Taylor, who was surprised and embarrassed. He explained that he remembered her mentioning at last year's holiday party that she did not drink; he thought it might be awkward to ask her to a happy hour. He felt terrible and sincerely apologized, and, of course, said that it would be great if she joined them. Aisha was relieved and appreciative of Taylor's apology and sincere invitation.

In his attempt to be sensitive to Aisha, Taylor had actually left her confused and upset. Imagine the potential long-term hurt and resentment she might have felt had she not taken the initiative to have the conversation. Also, recognize that Aisha's upset could have been avoided altogether if Taylor had been willing to have what he feared would be an awkward conversation about whether she would like to join the team at these gatherings.

Team-Level Impact

When two colleagues are in conflict, it adversely affects the whole team. This is especially true when the situation is widely known, as it usually is because each team member typically speaks poorly about the other. Team members may feel compelled to choose sides, and, in fact, may literally be asked to do so with phrases such as "Can I count on you to have my back?" Other team members get frustrated that their colleagues are unwilling to manage their differences maturely and professionally. Conflict that began between two people often creates negative feelings and friction across an entire team. As a result, communication and collaboration break down and are sometimes never fully restored. Consider the following example.

I was once asked to work with Carlos, the head of business development, and Sofia, a senior salesperson, who had not spoken for several months. They worked in a satellite office of a global company with a total of nine employees. Apparently, Sofia had sold new business to an existing customer that Carlos felt should have fallen under business development. (He was upset that he did not make the commission.) Whether intentional or not, Sofia had not kept Carlos informed about the deal, and he was blindsided during a meeting with the client, which put him in an awkward and embarrassing situation. Carlos was furious. He and Sofia had a very unhealthy conversation that resulted in a complete refusal by both to further communicate or collaborate. (They sent curt emails to one another when absolutely necessary or asked colleagues to serve as go-betweens.)

The tension in the office was so thick that you could cut it with a knife. The manager was ineffectual and had done little more than ask them to try to get along. I spoke with the team members who were flat-out angry and fed up with the situation, especially when they were put in the middle. To state the obvious, Carlos and Sofia's dysfunctional relationship had a devastating effect on office morale, decreased communication and collaboration, and made for incredibly awkward team meetings. As is usually the case, Sofia and Carlos had little appreciation for the negative impact their dispute was having on their colleagues. Fortunately, after discussing the issue, they became receptive to working with me and with each other. It took a day and a half of in-person meetings, as well as follow-up phone coaching, but the investment was worthwhile, as they subsequently were able to maintain a professional, respectful, and collaborative working relationship.

Organization-Level Impact

An organization's ability to function at a high level and satisfy customers' needs depends on healthy relationships among team members. Strife between coworkers diminishes efficiency, productivity, and quality work. *You cannot have excellent external customer service without excellent internal customer service.* Consider the following example of how conflict can adversely impact customers and organizations.

Kaitlyn, a production manager, and Samir, a sales manager, had worked relatively well together for about three years. However, in the past nine months their relationship had grown progressively more contentious. Samir was under tremendous pressure to deliver numbers in a very challenging environment, and, in several instances, made promises to clients that Kaitlyn's team simply could not reasonably meet. Kaitlyn asked Samir multiple times to please consult her about production and shipping schedules. She told me that she had bent over backward time and again to accommodate Samir, including paying employees for overtime, which hurt her budget.

One day, an important client received a shipment of goods that was 30 percent less than expected. Samir got a call from his irate customer who had been counting on those parts to fulfill one of his client's orders. Kaitlyn was well aware of the partial shipment but had purposely kept that information from Samir. She felt that enough was enough, and this was the only way to teach him a lesson and get him to start respecting her and her needs. Surprise, surprise, Kaitlyn and Samir's relationship continued to deteriorate and the customer took his business elsewhere.

Organizational Values and Culture

When it comes to healthy relationships and conversations, there is one important topic that never seems to get attention, namely, the role of an organization's core values and culture.

Corporate values are intended to drive the behaviors and attitudes that comprise a company's culture, which then reinforces the values over time. For example, if a company wishes to promote a culture of collaboration, then teamwork would likely be a core value. If you want a culture in which team members deal with conflict in a straightforward and respectful manner, then you need core values that hold people accountable to such behaviors. Unfortunately, what is quite simple in theory often does not work well in practice. In reality, an organization's culture can be a far cry from its core values, and often for the worse.

There are three primary reasons why core values do not have greater influence on organizational culture. First, they tend not to be well defined. For example, a company that identifies "respect" as a core value might describe it as "Respect for our team members and our customers." That sounds nice but is extremely vague. It is difficult to hold people accountable to nebulous statements. Core values should have clear behaviors associated with them. Continuing to use respect as the example, take a few moments and jot down some behaviors associated with demonstrating this value in the workplace. How did you do? Did you write down any of the following?

- Always be on time for meetings and come fully prepared.

- Ask the person who tends to say the least in a meeting to share her thoughts first.

- Respond quickly to messages.

- Give clear feedback in a supportive and constructive manner.

- Give colleagues as much advance notice as possible when you will need something from them.

Many people find this exercise quite challenging. Over the years, I have developed a list of 100-plus behaviors associated with fostering a respectful and collaborative workplace environment. (If you are interested in receiving this list, email me at: Paul@PaulMarciano.com.)

The second reason that core values do not have much impact on culture is that they are hardly ever referenced or reinforced beyond the employee handbook, company website, and a few posters. Core values should be splashed everywhere. Every company's internal communication and marketing department should have a strategy that promotes its core values. Whenever I walk into a client's office for the first time, I immediately search for where their values are posted. Ideally, it begins with them prominently displayed in the reception area. If I were to walk into your company, how long would it take me to discover your corporate values? Not to embarrass you, but do you even know them? Sadly, most employees in most companies do not.

Third, even when the core values are well known and under-stood, it is the exceptional organization where employees are actually held accountable to them. Huber is one such company. Founded in 1883, Huber considers four principles the bedrock of its organization: Respect for People, Ethical Behavior, Excellence, and Environmental, Health, Safety, and Sustainability. As should be the case in all organizations, these values are incorporated into employees' performance reviews. All leaders are expected to serve as role models and are held accountable for being so. If you do not live by the Huber principles, then you do not work at Huber. If you are interested in having a company that spans three centuries, pay attention to your values and principles, and hold people responsible to living them.

Shin and Madison were department managers whose organization touted "collaboration" and "respect" as core values. It said so on the website. Unfortunately, Shin and Madison apparently had not been on the website for months because their behavior ran quite counter to these values. They continually spoke poorly about one another, pointed fingers, exhibited passive-aggressive behavior such as not responding to emails, publicly argued, criticized the work and suggestions of the other, and even attacked each other's character. They were role models for how to *devalue* one another and their organization's values.

In speaking with their boss, Nia, I asked why she had allowed such behavior to continue. She responded, "I've talked to them several times, and they seem to get better for a while. They are effective managers, and, honestly, I really don't want to lose either of them."

I replied, "But you're OK with potentially losing your company's values?" In general, managers often tolerate poor behavior because, in their minds, it is an either/or proposition: they either allow employees to act as they are, or risk losing them. This is a false premise intended to rationalize avoiding doing one's job and dealing with the situation. It is my sincerest hope that this book will help managers address instances in which employee behavior is compromising their company's values. Core values must be nonnegotiable.

SUMMARY

As you can see, conflict between two people can have a widespread impact on other team members, customers, and the organization. I view avoiding difficult conversations as selfish and irresponsible because it detracts from employees' ability to fulfill their company's mission. Choosing not to communicate or collaborate with a team member is unacceptable because it limits your effectiveness and that of your coworkers. Do the right thing and be committed to having a healthy conversation and restoring respect to the relationship. Not only will this make you feel empowered and decrease the stress in your life, but it will also have positive benefits on your fellow team members and your company as a whole.

UP NEXT

Most of us are aware we have biases that impact how we view others and the world. Unfortunately, most people do not know the extent to which unconscious biases affect our relationships. The next chapter may be very eye-opening. Please avoid becoming defensive or pretending that you are not biased. Instead, work to understand the impact of your biases and seek to overcome them.

ON YOUR PLAYING FIELD

1. Think about conversations you are currently avoiding or have avoided in the past and the negative impact doing so has had on you, the other person, your team, your customers, and the overall organization. In light of your responses, do you still think that ignoring a problem and holding a grudge with a colleague is in anyone's best interest? Or do you think it might be selfish and unprofessional behavior? If it were your company, would it be OK with you to have two employees refuse to work together?

2. When it comes to clearly tying behaviors to core values, how would you rate your organization? If the answer is "Not so well," then begin by forming a cross-functional team to identify the desired behaviors that go along with each value. Then think about what a team member would be saying and doing to reinforce the value.

CHAPTER 4

UNCONSCIOUS BIASES

Cognitive biases are mental filters that significantly impact our perception and interpretation of the world around us. These filters affect our thoughts, feelings, and actions. Over a hundred biases have been identified and are largely unconscious to us. The purpose of this chapter is to point out the biases that hinder our ability to have healthy conversations. As you read, consider how each colors the way in which you see others and the world.

Implicit Bias

Implicit bias is more commonly known as stereotyping. We stereotype when we ascribe certain traits and characteristics to groups of people globally. For example, "Americans are loud," "French people are rude," and "Germans have no sense of humor." From an evolutionary perspective, stereotyping impacts survival, as it allows us to quickly determine the extent to which others are "like us" and members of our tribe. Similarity is associated with safety, whereas dissimilarity is associated with a potential threat.

We stereotype people along all kinds of characteristics, most notably, gender, race, ethnicity, religious affiliation, age, sexual orientation, and socioeconomic status. Stereotyping is based on our direct and indirect experience with others. While we may not want to admit it, we are quite biased and prejudiced by both nature and nurture. To believe otherwise is evidence of our bias to always want to look good to ourselves and others. Rather, our goal should be to shine a light on our unconscious biases and examine how they influence what we think and do, particularly if they lead to discriminatory practices. In the following exercise, complete the sentence with whatever adjectives come immediately to mind:

- ▶ Politicians are:

- ▶ Vegetarians are:

- ▶ First responders are:

- ▶ Used car salesmen are:

- ▶ People with body piercings are:

- ▶ Librarians are:

- ▶ Doctors are:

- ▶ Yoga instructors are:

Notice how quickly and easily you were able to complete this exercise and stereotype groups of people, even if you have never met a member of that group. You may not personally know a politician, a vegetarian, or a yoga instructor, but that does not deter you from forming a clear opinion about "those kinds of people." That is a problem, especially if our thoughts lead us to judge others in a negative and critical manner. I can only imagine what you might think of a vegetarian used car salesman with body piercings!

We judge people all the time, instantaneously, while knowing nothing about them. Think about sitting at a traffic light when another car pulls up next to you. As you glance over, you might look at the make of the car, the driver, the driver's clothing, age, attractiveness, tattoos, and/or behavior (is the driver smoking, texting, singing out loud, screaming at children in the back seat?). Based on the appearance of the car and driver and the goings-on, you are going to make snap judgments about this person's character, wealth, status, and background. Obviously, if there is a golden retriever with her head hanging out the window, the driver is a good guy! By the way, if it hasn't occurred to you, this happens in reverse as well: people are stereotyping and judging you all the time. How does it feel?

Why Should We Care?

At the most basic level, stereotyping can demean, devalue, and degrade employees. It can also result in unfair employment practices, some of which are illegal. Stereotyping people leads to all sorts of assumptions about others' intelligence, skills, values, and work ethic. While stereotypes may apply to some members of a group, they rarely apply to all members and are typically exaggerated. The characterizations are commonly pejorative and can lead people to feel inferior, marginalized, and repressed. At the same time, it is important to point out that not all stereotypes might be considered negative or critical, in fact, sometimes they can be a blend of both positive and negative qualities. For example, someone who earned a doctorate from an Ivy League school might be simultaneously characterized as highly intelligent and an elitist snob with no common sense.

Stereotyping frequently results in people being disrespected, which can create conflict and make conversations more difficult. When you feel disrespected, you do not believe your opinions matter to the person or that you are a valued member of your team. Your comments, ideas, and actions are viewed through the lens of what "people like you" say and do. Let's look at a few examples.

Imagine a woman in a male-dominated industry like construction. Male colleagues may dismiss her opinions because, well, she is a female. Obviously, she will feel insulted. Hopefully, she will stand up for herself, which might ruffle some feathers and generate discord. Alternatively, perhaps a junior employee's suggestions are quickly rejected because of his youth and lack of experience. He may not even be asked for his opinions in the first place. Or how about a senior employee who is perceived as being stuck in the past and resistant to change? She might be left out of conversations about innovation and strategy, which might lead her to feel irrelevant and disrespected. Or a manager might get frustrated with a millennial team member because he considers her lazy, sensitive, and egocentric. Can you relate to any of these scenarios as either the one who is being stereotyped or the one stereotyping others?

The perception of being stereotyped can lead us to internalize the associated biases and influence how we think about ourselves and our abilities. When we are led to believe that "people like us" are not supposed to be adept at a particular skill, we underperform in that area. In their review article "Addressing Stereotype Threat Is Critical to Diversity and Inclusion in Organizational Psychology,"* Bettina Casad and William Bryant cite numerous findings that demonstrate the destructive impact of stereotyping in the workforce, including:

1. Minorities are more likely than non-minorities to view constructive feedback as negative, which may lead them to become defensive and less receptive to the very advice that may make them more effective and successful.

2. When individuals believe that their minority or stigmatized group is associated with poorer performance, they may disengage and reduce the amount of attention, care, and concern they show for their work.

3. When individuals feel that belonging to an identified group limits their career options, they are likely to reduce their efforts. Why bother working hard if my age, race, or gender is going to determine my success? For example, when an organization has primarily men in leadership roles, the message to women may be that they do not possess the characteristics necessary to be effective at such levels.

---

* B. J. Casad and W. J. Bryant, "Addressing Stereotype Threat Is Critical to Diversity and Inclusion in Organizational Psychology," *Frontiers in Psychology*, 7, no. 8 (2016), 1–18.

In *Blink*, Malcom Gladwell describes a scenario in which a white man is interviewing a black person:

> In all likelihood, you won't be aware that you're behaving any differently than you would around a white person. But chances are you'll lean forward a little less, turn away slightly from him or her, close your body a bit, be a bit less expressive, maintain less eye contact, stand a little farther away, smile a lot less, hesitate and stumble over your words a bit more, laugh at jokes a bit less. Does that matter? Of course it does. . . . [The candidate is] going to pick up on that uncertainty and distance, and that may well make him a little less certain of himself, a little less confident, and a little less friendly. And what will you think then? You may well get a gut feeling that the applicant doesn't really have what it takes, or maybe that he is a bit standoffish, or maybe that he doesn't really want the job.*

We also stereotype people based on their job function, which can have a profound impact on how those in different departments view one another. For example, "People in accounting are just number crunchers and don't understand how the business actually runs." "Upper management doesn't care about hourly employees." "Engineers think they are smarter than everyone else." "Salespeople only care about themselves." "The only thing human resources is good for is making more paperwork!"

Such characterizations create silos across departments that diminish communication and collaboration. We-versus-them attitudes are fostered, and "You don't understand or appreciate what we do" becomes a common refrain. Employees in different departments become jealous and distrustful, interdepartmental projects take longer, decisions are made with less or biased information, teams fight for

---

* M. Gladwell, *Blink: The Power of Thinking Without Thinking* (Little, Brown and Company, 2005), 85–86.

resources, and "blamestorming" (finger-pointing) becomes more prevalent than brainstorming. Overall, silos adversely impact productivity, efficiency, quality, relationships, and individual and team morale.

In addition to being the right thing to do, greater workplace diversity makes good business sense and has been associated with increased profits, lower turnover, higher levels of employee engagement, greater innovation, better decision-making, and a competitive edge when it comes to employee recruitment. There is no question that having a strong culture of diversity and inclusion makes a difference in the vitality of employees and organizations.

ON YOUR PLAYING FIELD

At this point, hopefully and unfortunately, you are keenly aware of human beings' default tendency to stereotype and judge others and the adverse impact of doing so. Take some time to consider the many ways in which stereotyping impacts you and others.

1. Have you ever made initial judgments about someone and later realized that you had completely mischaracterized him? How might you prevent doing so in the future?
2. Choose a stereotype that you hold about a group of people. What characterizations and assumptions do you make about people in this group (e.g., their work ethic, intelligence, judgment, open-mindedness, etc.)?
3. List three departments in your company. In general, how are they stereotyped? Objectively speaking, how accurate are these characterizations?
4. How do others characterize your department? (It may be interesting to ask colleagues in other departments this question.) What could you do to change how your department is perceived?

Confirmation Bias

Confirmation bias refers to our tendency both to seek information that reaffirms our existing beliefs and to avoid or dismiss information that opposes our views. Once we adopt a position, we continue to reinforce it by what we choose to pay attention to and how we interpret data. For example, we spend more time watching and agreeing with politicians whose views align with our own than those whose views we oppose. When we do come across news and rhetoric from those in the opposing political party, we dismiss them as untruths and propaganda.

Confirmation bias shows up in our interactions with colleagues, customers, and vendors. It manifests in the decisions we make and the positions we take every day. Imagine, for example, you have a coworker named Doran who you believe does not carry his weight. As a result, you are constantly paying attention to instances that reinforce this belief, like when he failed to finish the weekly report on time, ignored critical emails, or arrived late to the staff meeting and gave a slipshod presentation. Given that Doran is typically a slacker and underperforms, you would think that if he performed at a high or even acceptable level, you would really take note. Unfortunately, our brains do not work like that. We pay attention to what is *not* working in our environment more than what is. Trust me, you will notice the next time Doran drops the ball but, sadly, not when he gets it across the goal line. And the more you pay attention to poor behavior, the more of it you will get. Moreover, you will always relate to and treat Doran through your critical lens. *Remember this general rule: whether it is your coworker, spouse, child, or pet, you will never get the behavior you want by paying attention to the behavior you do not want.* It simply does not work that way.

As another example of work-related confirmation bias, imagine that you are part of a cross-functional team responsible for giving recommendations to the CEO on whether to establish a flexible stay-at-home work policy. Personally, you are a single parent with a long and stressful commute, and you feel very strongly that such a policy will boost employee morale and productivity. Many other companies have successfully transitioned to such a model, and employees at your company have ready access to all necessary remote technology. With such a biased mindset, you would seek out data and anecdotal evidence that aligns with your views, much as an attorney would in preparing her case. In contrast, there are obviously others who would strongly oppose such a decision based on their views. Who is "right" depends on the lens through which you see the situation; no view is more inherently "wrong" or "right" than the other.

ON YOUR PLAYING FIELD

1. Think about a firmly held belief or position about which you would say that your mind is made up and others might call you stubborn. How can you shine a light on this belief or position to look for unconscious biases and examine how it influences what you think and do?

2. Do you hold a negative view of a team member? Who is your Doran? Once identified, imagine becoming a detective and look for contradictory evidence. You are now debating for the other team. For example, as much as you believe Doran is flaky, find at least three instances in which he followed through as he promised. You get bonus points if you can identify a time when he went above and beyond. Is Doran *always* as you describe him?

3. If you really want to go further, *create* instances in which Doran can be successful. Include him in tasks for which he is both passionate and highly competent. Doran's success will allow you to acknowledge his accomplishments, and you will begin to see him in a more positive light.

Belief Perseverance

Most of us like to think that we are logical, reasonable, and certainly willing to change our minds when presented with clear data that proves our beliefs invalid. Unfortunately, this is not always the case. Unlike confirmation bias in which we selectively attend to or ignore data, belief perseverance refers to our tendency to persist in our beliefs, despite strong evidence to the contrary. Unfortunately, doing so can have dire effects. For example, despite a vast amount of research that the COVID-19 virus is deadly and that social distancing, handwashing, and wearing face masks are necessary to stop the spread, some people maintain that it is an overblown hoax or tied to some political conspiracy. Similarly, despite overwhelming research showing that climate change is real and the potential impact catastrophic, some individuals outright dismiss the consequences or even the validity of this issue.

The seminal research in this area was conducted by social psychologist Leon Festinger.* His most well-known study focused on a religious cult called the Seekers, who believed that God was going to send a flying saucer to save them from an apocalypse on December 21, 1954. Led by Dorothy Martin, the members' beliefs were so strong that they gave up all their worldly possessions and left their jobs and spouses. As you may have guessed, they were wrong. So how do you think they reacted? Brilliantly, they claimed that because of their devoutness and sacrifices, God had spared Earth. It would be the ultimate self-confrontation to acknowledge that they had given up everything for some out-of-this-world idea that never happened! As referenced in Chapter 2, Festinger's research led to his theory of cognitive dissonance, which allows us to psychologically resolve situations in which we made mistakes by claiming that we did not. Obviously, such a strategy can lead to all kinds of frustration and conflict with others whose understanding of the situation is grounded in facts and objective evidence.

---

* L. Festinger, H. W. Riecken, and S. Schachter, *When Prophecy Fails: A Social and Psychological Study of a Modern Group That Predicted the Destruction of the World* (Harper–Torchbooks, 1956).

In belief perseverance, people often double down on their decisions. Consider the following example: Ellen owned a midsized trophy and engraving company and was presented with the opportunity to buy out a competitor. She saw all kinds of synergies and possibilities. During the due diligence phase, her accountant pointed out blatant discrepancies in the company's books. Ellen dismissed his counsel, however, and decided to "go with her gut." As soon as the deal was inked, customers started calling asking about prepaid orders, and vendors came knocking with overdue invoices. As her accountant had cautioned, the cash flow numbers were inaccurate and several purchase orders disappeared. Frustrated customers went elsewhere and vendors refused to extend further credit. Holding steadfast to her belief that she had made a wise decision, Ellen continued to pour money and resources into the business, and blamed unforeseeable changes in market conditions for decreased sales. Eventually, she was forced to close the office and took a tremendous financial loss that nearly brought down her entire company.

We all make errors in judgment and mistakes; when you do, be willing to admit them and take a different course of action to avoid further detriment to yourself, those around you, and your company.

ON YOUR PLAYING FIELD

1. Have you ever made a bad decision but could not bring yourself to acknowledge it at the time, and, instead, convinced yourself it was prudent? What was the impact?
2. How might you identify when you are engaged in belief perseverance?
3. Have you ever been confronted with a colleague in such a state? If so, how did you try to deal with him or her? Were you successful? How might you handle the situation differently now?

Note: For the interested reader, an excellent resource on this topic is Carol Tavris and Elliot Aronson's book, *Mistakes Were Made (but Not by Me): Why We Justify Foolish Beliefs, Bad Decisions, and Hurtful Acts.*

Reactive Devaluation

Reactive devaluation asserts that we devalue proposals made by those we consider adversaries. There is no better example of this bias than how politicians often refuse to even entertain proposals initiated by those in opposing parties. Allow me a soapbox moment. Don't you find it interesting (read: maddening) that in every election cycle, those running for public office talk about the American people's frustration at the lack of collaboration in Washington, and yet it never improves? That is why a copy of this book is being sent to every member of the United States Senate. It would be wonderful if instead of all the rhetoric and finger-pointing that, politicians said to one another, "Let's talk about it," and had civil dialogue.

I am sure you can see how reactive devaluation plays out at work. The more we view someone as "on the other side," the less likely we are to agree with her views or assign credibility to her. If Malik from operations has a suggestion, Barb from accounting might judge it to be a bad idea just because it is coming from him. In fact, Barb doesn't even need to hear the idea to know it is flawed and unworthy of consideration! By the way, Malik probably feels the same way about Barb's suggestions. Notice how little effort we make even to understand the ideas of those we dislike. Reactive devaluation significantly increases the risk of conflict and eliminates just about any chance of collaboration and healthy conversation. To mitigate this bias, both people must first begin treating one another with respect and recognize that the organization needs them to be allies, not adversaries.

ON YOUR PLAYING FIELD

1. Is there someone at work you simply do not like and you feel does not like you? Someone with whom you always seem to be on opposite sides of the fence? If so, consider for a minute if reactive devaluation comes into play during your conversations.
2. Now, think about a time when your ideas were devalued by a coworker due to his feelings toward you rather than based on their merit. How did it make you feel?
3. Who is the person that you get along least well with at work or with whom you feel some sense of competition? Write down three things you like or respect about that person. (You can do it.) The next time you have a meeting with her, look back at what you wrote. When she speaks, force yourself to think of her as your valued team member. Also, remind yourself, and perhaps others, that the focus should be on coming up with the best ideas, regardless of their authorship.

Naive Realism

Similar to reactive devaluation, naive realism leads us to minimize the opinions of those with whom we disagree. This bias is rooted in the self-belief that we see the world as it truly is, and if people disagree with us, they must be misinformed or irrational. Often, we believe that we view the world objectively. Nothing could be further from the truth. Imagine a pot into which you place your age, race, ethnicity, gender, sexual preference, education, socioeconomic status, citizenship, whether you are a parent or sibling, religious affiliation, country of origin, and where you grew up. Then into that pot place all your life experiences and personality characteristics. Reach in, pull out a pair of glasses, and you will see the lens through which you see the world is as unique as your thumbprint. No one sees the world as you do, and you do not see the world as anyone else does. Your view is *a* view, not *the* view.

Of all the biases, naive realism may be the most ubiquitous. We are by nature egocentric; we view the world as though everyone experiences the same reality, which is not at all true. You can imagine that the root of much conflict—personal and professional—revolves around the failure to understand, accept, and address this bias. The key to dealing with naive realism is empathy, which we will talk about several times in the remainder of the book. First, you must recognize that yours is a singular, subjective view. Second, your view is no more right or wrong than someone else's. Third, you must sincerely desire and seek to understand matters from others' perspectives. Reverse role-playing can be an insightful exercise. For example, identify an issue relevant to several departments, and then have representatives of each department meet to discuss it. The key is that the representatives switch roles: the engineer is now a marketing specialist, the accountant adopts the perspective of human resources, and so on. Empathy is the antidote for naive realism and many other biases.

ON YOUR PLAYING FIELD

1. What do you think are the key influences that shape your worldview? Create a list of what it is that makes you unique: your cultural experiences/traditions, personality characteristics, religion, family life, hometown, and so on. Can you appreciate the true uniqueness of your lens?

2. Which coworker is most different from you, for example, in gender, ethnicity, age, department, position, personality, where they grew up, their level of education, religious and political affiliations, and so on? Do you think these differences ever impact how you each view a particular issue? Hopefully, the one thing that everyone has in common and should support is the mission of your company!

3. Take a minute and identify an issue about which you have been singularly-minded. Schedule time to speak with someone who comes at the issue from a very different perspective and simply ask questions to understand her viewpoints. For example, you feel strongly about flexible work hours and remote work, while a colleague believes that active collaboration and holding people accountable necessitates people being in the office together. Use the time to talk about each other's views and reasoning. Additionally, consider taking a few minutes to get to know more about your colleague on a personal level and look for opportunities to increase your sense of relatedness.

Relationship History Bias

For the record, I just coined this bias, and while there is some overlap with other unconscious biases, I believe it deserves to be recognized on its own. Actually, I think it explains quite a few of them. See what you think.

Our interactions with others take place within the context of all of our previous dealings. We have relationship history. If your history with a colleague is characterized by disagreement and arguing, that is naturally how you would approach future conversations. Think about the difference in your mindset and attitude when you see the phone ring and it is a friend versus a dreaded coworker. Or perhaps your boss asks to speak with you, and all you can think of is, *What have I done wrong?* The likelihood of a healthy conversation depends largely on the history of your relationship. Here are some of the common things we say to ourselves when forced to have a conversation with someone we do not like:

- I can't wait to hear what Mike is going to say next!

- Maria is going to say the same thing she always says.

- What does Jimmy want now?

- There Letitia goes again, just promoting her own agenda.

- Lorenzo sure loves to hear himself talk.

- Easy for her to say!

- Majid never listens to what anyone else has to say.

- She's an idiot!

- TJ should get out of his office and actually come down to the plant, so he has a clue as to what he is talking about.

- I wonder if Sasha really believes her own nonsense?

- Here goes 30 minutes of wasted time!

- I wonder what I should make for dinner.

This self-talk does not lend itself to healthy conversations where we listen respectfully from a place of curiosity and with a mindset of collaboration. If you want to hear what another has to say, start by not listening to yourself. Even better, start by changing the conversation you have with yourself. Take note of when your self-talk becomes negative or critical toward others.

ON YOUR PLAYING FIELD

1. Think about someone from your past or present with whom you have a poor relationship history. When you think about speaking with him, what thoughts about him and your interactions together come to mind?
2. What are the consequences of such distracting and biased thoughts? In comparison, what would be the benefits of listening attentively without judgment?
3. If you are interested in addressing this bias, try the following: Before speaking with an individual with whom conflict is likely, write down on a yellow sticky note and repeat three times: "I am committed to being a nonjudgmental team member who listens respectfully to my colleagues." Place the note within your view and read it to yourself whenever you feel a sense of frustration during the conversation. It works!

Blind Spot Bias

The final, and possibly most important bias is the blind spot bias: thinking that you have no biases. If you still believe that the way you view people, approach problems, make decisions, and see the world in general is completely objective, then I have done a terrible job! Identifying and addressing blind spots around your prejudices and biases is essential if you hope to be a better colleague and human being. To state the obvious, it is hard to uncover blind spots on your own. Perhaps what you have read so far and the exercises you have completed helped reveal some of your unconscious biases. Reading about them in a book and understanding them intellectually is great, but it will not make a difference unless that knowledge changes your thoughts and actions.

ON YOUR PLAYING FIELD

1. Review the list of biases and select the one that you feel interferes most with your ability to view things objectively and collaborate effectively with others.
2. Write this bias down along with a statement, such as the following: "This bias distorts my reality, and I am committed to eliminating it." Read it throughout your day; create a calendar alert to prompt you.
3. Whenever you find yourself getting into an argument or dismissing someone's views, check in with yourself and see if this bias is coming into play. If so, acknowledge to yourself the impact it is having and then choose to eliminate it from your thinking. Over time, you should see a steady decrease in how often you invoke this unconscious bias. When you are ready, move on and tackle another.

SUMMARY

With all these ingrained unconscious prejudices and biases, it can be hard to see things objectively. We often find it easier to identify faults in others before recognizing them in ourselves. Acknowledging and dealing with our biases will help us see them in others—but let us work on ourselves first! A nearly universal maxim is that the more we get to know others, the more we like them; this is due in large part to an increased level of relatedness and understanding. Commit to and invest in getting to know your colleagues. *If you find yourself in a tug-of-war, put down the rope and remember that you are supposed to be pulling in the same direction.*

UP NEXT

Are you a strong introvert trying to have a conversation with a big-mouthed extrovert? Are you struggling to deal with a narcissist or pessimist? Do you wonder how to deal with people who have very different personalities than your own? Well, let's talk about it . . .

CHAPTER 5

PERSONALITY TRAITS

As you might imagine, I have worked with many challenging people over 30 years. One of the most frustrating things a client will say is: "Well, that's just my personality." I tell clients that I am not interested in changing their personality and have no idea how to even do so. Rather, I am interested in helping people understand the adverse impact of their behaviors on others, their relationships, and the probability of having healthy conversations. I want people to take responsibility for their actions and to understand that they get to make choices about how they relate to and treat others. Their souls are not condemned to spend eternity denigrating, humiliating, and yelling at others. Screaming is unacceptable, even if you tell me that it is because you are passionate, or better yet, because it is the only way that people will listen to you. When people blame their poor behavior on their personality, I invariably share the following story. (Before reading it, a quick note: a phrenologist was a practitioner who determined one's psychological traits by feeling the bumps on one's head.)

Moses' portrait was brought to a king whose astrologers and phrenologists concluded that Moses was a cruel, greedy, craven, self-seeking man. The king, who had heard that Moses was a kindly, generous, and bold leader, was puzzled, and went to visit Moses. Upon meeting him, he saw the portrait was good and said, "My phrenologists and astrologers were wrong." But Moses disagreed, "Your phrenologists and astrologers were right. They saw what I was made of. What they couldn't tell you was that I struggled against all that and became what I am."

While I cannot attest to the veracity of this story, its message is as meaningful and important today as it was in ancient times. Personality traits cannot serve as excuses for poor behavior. We must all take responsibility for our actions and how they impact others, even if it requires personal struggle to improve.

Personality refers to traits, characteristics, and thought processes that lead us to react in a predictable and reliable manner. As you well know, some personalities make difficult conversations even more difficult. Most of us work around our more negative attributes, and we try to work around the negative characteristics of others. I had a client who always found himself in the midst of conflict and could not understand why. I told him plainly that it was because he came across as narcissistic, arrogant, and insensitive. Most people have blind spots when it comes to recognizing their negative attributes, although we are pretty good at spotting them in others. If people believe you to be arrogant, it does not matter that you view yourself as humble. The goal of this chapter is to provide you with strategies to deal effectively with coworkers' difficult personalities, but it is also an important opportunity, as it was with cognitive biases, to reflect on your own thoughts and actions. Some elements of your own personality may be contributing to the interpersonal conflict in your life.

I have been told at times that my approach to dealing with others can come across as manipulative. The intention behind the strategies I recommend is to influence others' behaviors in order to decrease conflict and increase collaboration. A thesaurus will tell you that influence and manipulation are synonyms—"manipulate" just gets a bad reputation because it has a sinister connotation. It is important to recognize that we are constantly influencing and manipulating others by what we say and do. In fact, it is our failure to fully understand that impact that gets us into trouble! While it is commonly said that we cannot change or control others' thoughts or behaviors, that statement is patently false. We do it all the time. Here is an overly simplistic example: Imagine that every morning you go into work and say hello to the receptionist and ask how he is doing. One day, you start ignoring him and walk past without so much as a glance. After a week of this behavior, do you think he will still greet you warmly? Nope. Do you think that his feelings toward you have changed? Absolutely. If you would like to test this theory, feel free to try it on a loved one. Or not.

Now imagine being in a meeting where someone you normally disagree with makes a suggestion and you say, "Madison, I really like where you're going with this. I have to admit, I hadn't thought of approaching the solution from that angle." Are you changing how Madison might normally think about you? And, critically, might it alter how she responds to one of your suggestions? In fact, could such a comment spark an improvement in your relationship and foster healthier conversations? Yes, yes, and yes. We unconsciously influence people all the time. In fact, you might consider our ignorance of doing so the mother of all unconscious biases. Why not have a better understanding of how our words and behavior impact others and then choose them thoughtfully and intentionally? Let me be clear. I am not suggesting in any way that you try to influence or manipulate people just for the sake of doing so, or simply because you want to get your way, and certainly not for nefarious purposes. When you seek to influence others, do so with the intention to foster healthy relationships and conversations. With all this in mind, let us get started.

Passive-Aggressive

Passive-aggressive people tend to agree with others and then engage in behaviors that undermine that agreement. Tactics associated with this personality include procrastination, showing up late to meetings, missing deadlines, being purposely inefficient, delivering poor quality work, being unresponsive, answering questions incompletely, pretending to be ignorant, communicating in an unclear manner, covertly undermining others, and sabotaging a plan or work process.

Approach

Attempting to collaborate with a passive-aggressive individual can be extremely frustrating. A classic example is when you ask such a person if anything is wrong and they say "No" when you know perfectly well that there is. (In general, do not ask a question that can be answered by yes or no if your hope is to have a productive conversation.) Calling the person out by saying, "I can tell something is wrong" usually does not work because it would require the other person to admit that she lied when she said nothing was wrong. If you observe a change in a person's behavior or demeanor, comment on it to open up a conversation. For example, "Eli, I've noticed that you've been quiet recently. In the last meeting you barely said a word, and you're always passionate about safety issues. I would appreciate talking about what's on your mind, especially if you are upset with me about something." If the person says that nothing is wrong or "I'm fine," you will likely want to leave it alone or invite future conversation by saying something along these lines, "OK. If something does come up, please let me know." If the atypical behavior continues or becomes more exaggerated, I recommend addressing the situation again. "Eli, ever since the last team meeting when I said that I disagreed with you, you've barely said a word to me. It seems pretty clear that you are upset with me, and I would like to speak with you about what happened."

Passive-aggressive people are quite skilled at making excuses, especially when you try to hold them accountable, for instance:

> **Stella:** "Luke, you said that you would get me the report by noon, and it is now five o'clock. Have you finished it?"
>
> **Luke:** "Oh, I'm sorry. I was waiting on you to send me that other information."
>
> **Stella:** "What information?"

Luke: "That report from last month."

Stella: "You never asked me about a report."

Luke: "Sure I did. I sent you an email about it yesterday."

Stella: "I never received an email from you."

Luke: "I'm sure I sent it. Let me check. Ugh, can you believe it got stuck in my draft folder?!"

Stella: (Thinking) Actually, yes.

Passive-aggressive types can be hard to hold accountable and can make you want to scream. If you are managing such people, the best approach is to set extremely clear and specific expectations. It is best to break assignments into mini-tasks, which will make it less likely for them to get "confused" about how to prioritize these, so you can ensure they stay on track. You should have regular check-ins at the beginning and end of each day. Make sure to document conversations and progress. Micromanaging people is a terrible idea, except in this instance.

In general, when dealing with passive-aggressive people, be extremely direct. Use simple, clear, and objective language; get their verbal agreement and commitment; and then follow up conversations with a detailed email breaking out specific deliverables and time frames. Provide examples of how you want things done, and direct them to contact you immediately with any problems. Request that they reply to your emails within 24 hours to acknowledge receipt and confirm understanding. Having discussions in the presence of other team members can be helpful in holding passive-aggressive people accountable.

Aggressive

Assertive, good. Aggressive, bad. For the most part, being assertive is a positive personality trait, especially in the workplace. To the left of assertive is passive, which can definitely serve as a limiting factor in one's career. A passive person's voice is less likely to be heard in general, but especially in the presence of an aggressive colleague. Aggressiveness is rarely a positive attribute, unless it is the cultural norm of an organization. Exceptions aside, aggressive behavior can make others feel attacked and triggers the fight-or-flight response, neither of which contribute to collaboration or healthy conversations. This personality attribute is a huge blind spot. During a 360-degree assessment, I can interview a dozen people who all characterize an individual as aggressive, and yet the individual himself will identify as assertive.

Approach

In my experience, aggressive people are accustomed to getting their way because they intimidate others. While you do not have to become aggressive yourself when working with such a person, you should be firm and stand your ground. Creating a time-out can be an extremely effective technique. A friend of mine, Annalisa, worked in a construction company where assertiveness was the norm and aggressiveness readily tolerated. When Annalisa tried to discuss an issue with a colleague, he became highly agitated and started ranting. Annalisa said, "Ted, you're not going to yell at me. I came to you to have a conversation. When you're ready to have a conversation, please give me a call." Annalisa spoke calmly, confidently, clearly, and concisely. She created a time-out that provided Ted the opportunity to calm down. She also put the responsibility on him to reach out when he was ready, which he did two hours later, and they had a very productive discussion. In case you're wondering, Ted did not apologize. However, it is likely that he respected Annalisa more for standing up for herself and calling him out for his unacceptable, noncollegial behavior.

When it comes to discussing matters with an aggressive person, I prefer group settings where reasonable team members can dilute the voice and opinions of their forceful colleague. Ideally, team members have one another's back, so if the aggressive person targets an individual and her ideas, another team member will step up and show support for the colleague. There is strength in numbers, and an aligned group of coworkers can surmount the behavior of a single aggressive team member. Since aggressive people dominate conversations, during a meeting you might suggest going around the room and giving everyone five minutes to present their thoughts without interruption. Nonverbal behavior such as looking down and remaining expressionless can help to extinguish inappropriate behavior. I suggest documenting any aggressive behavior, as it will be useful should you decide or need to file a complaint. Obviously, if you feel at all threatened by the individual, you should immediately report him to human resources.

Arrogant

Arrogant individuals are narcissistic and consider themselves superior to colleagues in terms of their intelligence, skills, and value to the organization. They tend to be condescending, disrespectful, dismissive, and often feel and act entitled. In fact, some arrogant people are unabashed in sharing how talented and special they are. Obviously, they are not ideal collaborators because they believe their ideas are better than those of others. Arrogant people are, however, adept at offending colleagues and breeding animosity in the workplace. Of course, the opposite of arrogance is humility, which is one of the most crucial characteristics of any good team member. And when it comes to being an effective leader, self-confidence is critical because no one wants to follow a leader who does not believe in herself. However, too much self-confidence can come across as arrogance. The objective is to come across as self-confident *and* humble.

Approach

Arrogant people are all about impressing other people and looking good. Their image matters most, so you never want to say anything in a public setting that could cause them embarrassment, unless you want to start a war. Given my stance for respect in the workplace and world, arrogant people and their sense of superiority push my buttons big-time. Having said that, dealing with such people is not particularly difficult because you know exactly what drives them: their ego. Ask them lots of questions and give them plenty of room to talk, especially about their accomplishments. Make statements that show respect and deference for their intelligence, good judgment, and character. Avoid talking about yourself unless it makes the other person feel or look good—for example, "I would never have thought of such an out-of-the-box solution." While you risk biting your lip so hard that you taste blood, stroking an arrogant person's ego will likely lead to a halo effect resulting in her having positive feelings toward you.

Imagine working for an egotistic manager who is constantly critical of your work, and you want to discourage the constant critique. You might try saying something like: "Leon, I am sorry that I am not meeting your expectations. I know that you can run this piece of equipment with your eyes closed, but I simply don't have your skills or experience. I want to do a good job, and I hope that you can see that. I know how busy you are managing the entire department, but I would greatly appreciate your teaching me how to better dial in the specs to avoid quality defects." While all this may come across to you as insincere and manipulative, I am suggesting such an approach to avoid conflict and promote collaboration. I am recommending it because it will make your life easier.

Self-Focused

Self-focused people tend to be egocentric, self-absorbed, and selfish. They are concerned with and consumed by their own well-being and give little thought to the welfare of fellow team members. To get their needs met, they will exaggerate, exert pressure, and even lie; in fact, they may feel justified in behaving in these ways. In *SuperTeams*, I refer to such individuals as TeamMe vs. TeamWe players. People who are self-focused differ from arrogant people; self-focused team members don't care how they come across—so long as they get what they want.

Approach

When dealing with self-focused people, concentrate on how you can best support them and their agenda. Do not mention your own needs, even if they align with theirs. In fact, it may actually annoy them if you say, "Yes, that works for me." Remember, it is all about them. When self-focused people make a request, paraphrase it back to them. Begin with, "I want to be certain that I am clear about what you need from me . . ." They want to know that you understand the importance and urgency of their needs. Someone with this personality might say, "You have to understand that my work is critical and has to take precedence over that of others." You might respond, "I'm glad you explained to me how critical this work is."

Self-focused people want to be accommodated, so when they make a request, act as though you are doing them a favor, whether or not you are. For example, imagine Trevon comes to you on a Monday and tells you that he needs your team to work on a project starting on Wednesday—which simply is not possible. If you are trying to avoid conflict and foster collaboration, try this:

> Trevon, I'm really glad you let me know how important this project is. I wish I had known even sooner so I could have planned my team's work around your needs. Let me see what I can do in terms of moving some of my people around and pushing back less urgent deadlines. I may be able to get someone working on this early next week. (Know in your mind that you can get to it sooner.)

Your follow-up conversation might go:

> Trevon, I let everyone on the team know your work is a priority. We were able to push some work back and get creative in terms of scheduling. Scott even said he would be willing to put in overtime to help you out. So, the good news is that we can begin working on your project this Friday.

As I am sure you have experienced, self-focused people make these last-minute requests all the time. When you acquiesce, you reinforce bad behavior, so it is important to address the issue and communicate that it will be better for *him* if he can give you more of a heads-up going forward. For example:

> Trevon, I am committed to delivering what you need, when you need it. I know that emergencies come up, and, when they do, my team and I try to be as responsive and accommodating as possible. However, the only way to ensure that you will be able to meet the demands of your customers is to get the order to me at least a week in advance.

If you have already had this conversation (you probably have many times) and he continues to make such last-minute requests, you are going to have to stand your ground at some point. Your decision to do so may lead to a confrontation, which, fortunately, you will know how to deal with more effectively by the end of the book.

Suspicious

Suspicious people lack trust and believe that others have ulterior motives. They are skeptical and cynical, and may even be paranoid. Such individuals are likely to be guarded and indirect in their communication. They worry about being taken advantage of and seek to limit any vulnerabilities. Naturally, it takes a long time to build a trusting relationship with a suspicious person, and any hint of disloyalty or subconscious feeling that "something isn't right" will take trust down to zero. I once asked a client who had tested high on suspiciousness what someone could do to gain his trust. His response: "Nothing."

Approach

Naturally suspicious people can be extremely difficult to collaborate with because they are not forthcoming with information. They are inclined to believe that you are not being fully transparent and may be seeking to take advantage of them. While their behavior does not foster collaboration, they are more likely to withdraw than to become aggressive. As soon as they sense any kind of deception, disagreement, or conflict, they immediately shut down and focus on reducing their vulnerabilities. Think of a turtle receding into its shell. Communication essentially ceases, which means, of course, that any unresolved conflict will remain unresolved. It can become very frustrating and tiring to deal with such people as you must worry about everything you say and how you say it.

When dealing with distrusting people, be overly transparent and direct. Doing so reduces wariness. If you disagree with a suspicious person, be straight about it. For example, "I do not agree with you on that point" is clear, is devoid of emotion, and gets to the heart of the matter. When you agree with the individual, state that as well. You want to limit the extent to which a suspicious person thinks to herself, *I wonder what he really thinks.* As always during a difficult conversation, it is helpful to remain focused on areas of agreement and alignment, no matter how small. With distrustful people, email is often the preferred mode of communication because this allows them to carefully craft their responses and take comfort in knowing that all discussions are documented. Of course, they will completely obsess about whatever you write.

Like respect, giving trust can help you receive it in turn. You might say, "Eva, I know that I can trust you and would like to share something in confidence with you." If the other person perceives that you are vulnerable, all the better, because it may help her feel she has the upper hand. Obviously, if you do not actually trust the other person, use good judgment in what you share. If you sense that the other person is shutting down and becoming defensive, address it outright by saying, "I am concerned that I may have said or done something that you find unsettling. May I ask what that is?" Or, "It looks like this situation is really pitting our interests against one another. I'd like to discuss how we might be able to eliminate that and seek a compromise." It can be very difficult to earn the trust of a wary individual. Just continue to be clear, transparent, and consistent. When it comes to decisions, give the suspicious person the time and space she needs to process information; never make her feel pressured. Being a distrusting, paranoid, and highly suspicious person is a tough way to live, so I remind myself to be empathetic in my dealings with such an individual.

Pessimist

Pessimists are cynics and doubters, about anything and everything. They view the world through a negative lens; the glass is always half empty. Small concerns can become exaggerated and catastrophic thinking may kick in. Some statements a pessimist may make include "There is no way we are going to win that bid," "The chances of that solution working are zero," and "I heard that our client was talking to a competitor. We are definitely going to lose him." Unfortunately, like a dark cloud, their negativity often influences colleagues and decreases team morale. Obviously, this is a terrible trait for a manager.

Approach

Pessimists are fond of the phrase "No, that won't work." The optimist's response of "Sure it will" will only be met with resistance. A pessimist views an optimist as unrealistic and impractical. When you find yourself in such a verbal tug-of-war, a good strategy is to agree with the pessimist. For example, "Adrian, actually, I agree with you. I don't think the plan is going to work *as it stands*." Make sure not to connect the two sentences with the word "but." The words "as it stands" are key because you can now continue the conversation by considering alternatives. Obviously, it is critical to sincerely seek to understand the pessimist's objections and point of view. For example, "Adrian, I would really like to understand from your perspective what specific aspects of the plan you feel won't work." If you are confronted with, "All of it," do not give up. Pick the smallest, most basic aspect of the situation or plan with which the other person would have a hard time disagreeing. For example, "Based on our last conversation with the client, would you agree that he isn't satisfied with our work? [Yes.] From what I heard him say, he wanted us to come up with solutions. Before we put forth any options, it seems that it would be helpful to arrange a call between the client's engineers and ours to ensure that we fully understand the issues. Does that seem reasonable?" Getting that first yes is critical.

When interacting with a pessimist, a good general rule is to ignore critical comments or counteract them. Do not let yourself get pulled into the negativity vortex. If someone sarcastically says to me, "Good luck with that!" I usually say in a very sincere manner, "Thank you. I really appreciate your support." I then quickly walk away. If someone makes a generally negative comment such as, "It is such a miserable day outside," I might respond, "We sure are lucky we don't live just a few miles north, or we would be getting sleet instead of rain," or "I hear that it is supposed to turn sunny over the next few days." In many cases, especially if the comment is a negative one about a coworker, the best approach is simply to ignore it. For example, if I were on a Zoom call and a colleague texted me something critical about another colleague's contributions, I simply would not respond. In general, give as little attention as possible to negative comments or you may inadvertently reinforce them.

Closed-Minded

Closed-minded individuals are only interested in keeping things as they are. To them, change is bad. Such people are fond of saying, "Don't fix what isn't broken" and "That is not how we do things around here." As a result, closed-minded people also tend to be characterized as "old school" and stubborn. As with the pessimist, alternate views are shot down without any real thought or discussion. Dealing with closed-minded people can be quite frustrating; having a healthy conversation or compromising is not possible when they do not want to have a conversation at all!

When you are closed-minded, you are closed off to new ideas and potentially more efficient and effective ways of doing your job, managing your people, or running your business. I find business founders and owners particularly prone to ignoring the opinions of others, among whom there is no better example than Henry Ford. In his book *Forbes Greatest Business Stories of All Time*, Daniel Gross details the incredible rise of the Ford Motor Company and its steep decline due to Henry Ford's unwillingness to listen to anyone's counsel other than his own.* For more than a quarter of a century, Ford sold its black Model T with few changes. Those around Ford kept encouraging him to innovate, but he would have none of it. Once, when he was away on vacation, his employees took the initiative to build an updated Model T. What was Ford's response? Legend has it that he smashed in the windshield and stomped on the roof. In the 1920s General Motors began to overtake Ford with its inexpensive and better-styled and equipped Chevrolet models. By 1926, sales of the Model T had plummeted. It was only thanks to Ford's son Edsel, who had surreptitiously collected designs for the Model A, that the company was saved. Henry Ford nearly caused the demise of his own company—one of the greatest, most significant and iconic companies in American history—because of his unwillingness to listen to others. If you want to be a great leader, learn to be a great listener and to value the ideas of your loyal employees, no matter their position.

Approach

Conflict with closed-minded people typically arises when changes are introduced because changes present uncertainty and cause anxiety. This is especially true when people fear that they and/or their roles are at risk of becoming less relevant. When dealing with such people, empathy is crucial. Put yourself in their shoes and view the situation from their perspective. Might you be concerned that your job responsibilities will shift and you will no longer be successful in

---

* Daniel Gross, *Forbes Greatest Business Stories of All Time* (John Wiley & Sons, 1996).

the new role? That you will end up losing autonomy and decision-making authority? That you will be reassigned to a new team when you have built good relations with your current colleagues? As human beings, we focus more on the potential downside rather than potential benefits of change, especially when those changes are imposed on us.

When dealing with closed-minded individuals, the first step is to engage them in conversation and facilitate their receptivity to discussing the issue and possible options. For example, "Benita, I was hoping to get your thoughts on reconfiguring the production line. As the lead tech, you know the process better than anyone. What is working well, and what is not working well? What causes the biggest headaches and frustrations for the team?" Ask Benita questions that encourage big-picture thinking rather than focusing on minor tweaks. For example, "If you were to start from scratch and build out an entirely new process, what might that look like?" Often, people ingrained in doing work a certain way for a long period of time do not have a vision of how things might operate differently. If possible, expose the individual to different models—for example, take them on physical or virtual tours of facilities that utilize alternative approaches to completing similar work and allow them to ask questions of the operators. Doing so serves as a learning opportunity and makes options real and not just theoretical. When the individuals do explore other options, make sure to thank them for their willingness to do so. Being as concrete and specific as possible in terms of how the changes will impact the individual and team will likely reduce angst. Obviously, seek to identify and discuss likely positive outcomes—all the better if you ask questions that lead the closed-minded person to identify any positive consequences of the change.

Another tactic to open up dialogue is to bring up new or recent influences that impact the business but have not been addressed, for example, "Given recent changes in technology, expanded product lines, and increased competition, do you think it makes sense to examine how we currently do things and look for opportunities to make improvements? Do you see any downside to doing so?" During conversations with closed-minded individuals, ask lots of "what-if" questions, listen, and paraphrase. Brainstorm options and fully explore the upside and downside of each, including the option of not making any changes. Treat the other person's concerns as valid and never minimize them. Instead of saying, "You're focusing on something that really isn't relevant," try, "I want to make sure I understand how that issue would impact the process overall and discuss how we might address it." The more input people have in decisions, the more ownership they will take and the less resistance you will face.

Volatile

Several years ago during a workshop, a woman raised her hand and said, "How should I handle dealing with a crazy boss?" I asked if she could be more specific, and she went on to describe an individual whose behavior was erratic, unpredictable, illogical, angry, paranoid, and egocentric. I gave the only sensible, realistic response: "Good luck." Such a boss may come across as Jekyll and Hyde; sometimes she is super supportive and positive, and the next minute she is angry and screaming. She might tell you to do something one way and then berate you for doing so; when you remind her that you were just following her instructions, she holds firm that she never said anything of the sort. Unfortunately, I imagine that you have come across at least one person in your career or personal life that you would dub "crazy."

Approach

I honestly have only one piece of advice: to the extent possible, avoid such people in any part of your life. In the midst of a confrontation, simply try to placate him and extricate yourself from the situation. In general, try not to be alone during a highly emotional conversation with such an individual. Make sure to document all inappropriate behavior. If your job requires you to deal with this person on a regular basis and your manager and/or human resources is aware of the situation and does nothing about it, look for another job opportunity. The common and unfortunate reality is that the individual's inappropriate behavior is not news to anyone. Such a person is typically kept on because of a perceived difficult-to-replace skill set or because they are responsible for generating considerable revenue.

SUMMARY

This chapter has touched on a handful of personality traits; there are many more that individually and collectively influence our interactions with others. We cannot change our own personalities, let alone those of others, so we must become aware of how traits influence behavior and make choices in how we act and react to decrease the likelihood of conflict and increase the likelihood of collaboration.

UP NEXT

How you say something matters just as much as what you say. In the next chapter we will explore the nonverbal aspects of language and how it influences collaboration and confrontation.

ON YOUR PLAYING FIELD

1. Which of the traits discussed in this chapter do you see in yourself, even a little?
2. What behaviors are associated with these aspects of your personality and how do you think they impact others?
3. How might you better manage those negative behaviors?
4. Identify a colleague you would label with one of the personality traits discussed and with whom you tend to have conflict. Based on the strategies and examples in this chapter, how might you deal with that individual more effectively?

CHAPTER 6

NONVERBAL COMMUNICATION

Nonverbal communication refers to the transmission of information apart from spoken words, and includes facial expressions, gestures, personal space, and tone of voice. While nonverbal communication is a critical component of how we send and interpret messages, the oft-cited statistic that 93 percent of communication is nonverbal (55 percent is attributed to body language and 38 percent to vocal qualities) is, quite frankly, absurd. This myth arose out of research conducted in the 1960s by Professor Albert Mehrabian at UCLA, which included two very limited studies in which subjects were asked to interpret emotions behind single, spoken words and guess a woman's emotion from a photograph. In the words of Philip Yaffe, "There are certain 'truths' that are *prima facie* false. And this [the 7 percent rule] is one of them."* Nonverbal communication matters, and in some situations matters a lot, but to say that only 7 percent of communication is derived from the spoken word is simply untrue.

We use nonverbal cues to express meaning beyond words alone, and sometimes in place of them. To make a point emphatically, we

---

* P. Yaffe, "The 7% Rule: Fact, Fiction, or Misunderstanding," *Ubiquity*, October 2011, p. 3.

might raise our arms and move our hands in cadence with our voice. We might look down when we say something sad or shrug our shoulders when we are unable to answer a question. If we are upset, we might point our finger at someone, raise our voice, stare intently, or crowd someone else's physical space. Of course, these nonverbal cues must be interpreted with an understanding of our relationship with the other person and the context of the conversation. Relationship history bias plays a significant role when it comes to how we interpret others' nonverbal cues. For example, if we have historically disagreed with someone, we might interpret a certain facial expression as a frown that might register as neutral if a friend were to make the same expression.

Accurately interpreting and using nonverbal communication is a skill that can be honed and practiced. You can imagine how useful such a skill would be during a difficult conversation; being able to detect when people's spoken language does not match their nonverbal messaging is critical to understanding a conversation's full context. People with high levels of emotional intelligence (EQ) are most likely to pick up on these cues, though this chapter will help you interpret, understand, and use nonverbal communication even if your EQ is not particularly high. As you read, think about your own nonverbal communication style and how it influences others' interpretation of what you say, especially during difficult conversations.

Facial Expressions

The seminal research on facial expressions was conducted in the 1960s by American psychologist Paul Ekman, who identified six basic human emotions: anger, fear, disgust, happiness, sadness, and surprise. However, more recent research suggests that these basic emotions can be combined to create an additional 16 distinct expressions.* For example, imagine a friend walking into a surprise birthday party. Hopefully,

---

* S. Du, Y. Tao, and A. M. Martinez, *Compound Facial Expressions of Emotion*, Proceedings of the National Academy of Sciences, first published March 31, 2014, https://doi.org /10.1073/pnas.1322355111.

her face will tell you that she is both surprised and happy. Our facial expressions are readily and, often, accurately assessed by others. It is important to be cognizant of the faces that we naturally make when we are upset or angry, so that we might control them to avoid escalating conflict during a contentious conversation. For example, if someone says something with which you strongly disagree, it would be much more productive to put on a curious face rather than a critical, are-you-kidding-me face. (While not an empirically validated expression, I am guessing you have seen that one before.)

Of course, in addition to assessing facial expressions, we get all kinds of information from discrete facial regions, primarily from the eyes. Imagine someone staring at you intently. Depending on the person, the situation, and your state of mind, such a gaze may be construed as intimate or hostile. What does it mean when you are talking and someone turns his eyes away from you? Do you interpret such behavior as indicative of rudeness, boredom, shyness, disinterest, or disrespect? If we are in an argument and the other person looks down, does that mean that we have "won"? Does it mean anything at all? We break eye contact for many reasons, including when we process information, recall an incident, attempt to figure out how to respond to a question, or try to remember the name of that new intern. Whenever we begin thinking about such issues that require our focus, we shift our gaze away from the other person. Additionally, breaking eye contact is a cultural norm in Western society.

What meanings do we assign to raised eyebrows, blinking, squinting, tearing, or shifting eyes; pursed, upturned, or down-turned lips; or the crinkling of a nose? Do we construe these as expressions of curiosity, sadness, surprise, guilt, anger, upset, or agreement? And what do we do with information that we have processed instantly and unconsciously? How does it influence our feelings, thoughts, and actions? Does it lead us to behave in a manner that fosters collaboration or fuels conflict? What if our read is totally off? The speaker may have meant one thing and our biases had us interpret something entirely differently. The point of these questions is to make you consider all the stories we make up based on relatively minor facial expressions and the tremendous influence they can have on the course and outcome of a critical conversation. My strong advice when we do not know what other people are thinking, especially when verbal and nonverbal behavior do not seem aligned, is to ask them. For example, we might say, "Did I say something to upset you?" or "I'm wondering what you're thinking," or "Did you have a comment?" Choosing to interpret subtle signs and speculate about another's thoughts may make for an interesting game, but certainly does not make for healthy conversations.

There are, of course, micro-expressions that can communicate a more positive, curious, and happy attitude toward the other person and discussion. Facial expressions consistent with such feelings include a relaxed jaw, cheeks raised in a smile, the corners of lips drawn, crow's feet near the outside of the eyes, and wrinkles that run from the outer nose to the outer lip.* Once you become aware of such expressions, you can work to control them. In the words of Charles Darwin, "Every true or inherited movement of expression seems to have had some natural and independent origin. But when once acquired, such movements may be voluntarily and consciously employed as a means of communication."[†] In addition to being able to control your own expressions, you will also become more attuned to those of others. Coupled together, these two skills will make you a more sensitive, active listener.

What is the impact of someone who exhibits very limited facial expressions? Having a poker face is great when you are playing poker, but not so desirable when you are speaking with a colleague or direct report. As human beings, we have a desperate need to know what others are thinking, and it is actually quite unnerving to see no emotion on a person's face. When people do not say anything with their verbal or nonverbal behavior, we, unfortunately, tend to imagine them having negative and critical thoughts. Managers who exhibit

---

* V. V. Edwards, "The Definitive Guide to Reading Microexpressions (Facial Expressions)," *Science of People*, June 10, 2020, https://www.scienceofpeople.com/microexpressions/.
[†] M. Bates and P. S. Humphrey, *Charles Darwin: An Anthology* (Transaction Publishers, 2009), p. 395.

little emotion and are also not verbally expressive can cause considerable angst for their direct reports. In general, the less feedback a manager gives employees, the more anxiety it causes because they are unsure where they stand. The old-school, if-you-don't-hear-from-me-everything-is-fine management approach is particularly ineffective and demotivating for younger generation employees who expect regular feedback; when they do not hear from their boss they are likely to believe that they are not doing well. If you are someone who displays little emotion, it is important that you share your thoughts and feelings with others, either verbally or in writing, so that they do not end up scratching their heads and making up stories.

My client Alex was a very successful IT executive whom I had the pleasure of coaching. What makes Alex's story so relevant to this chapter is that he is legally blind. As is common, I began the engagement by conducting a 360-degree assessment, and the results were very revealing. Obviously, Alex did not have access to others' nonverbal communication; however, what I did not anticipate was how the lack of awareness of his own nonverbal behavior impacted others.

Alex was the opposite of poker-faced. His facial expressions clearly communicated—often in an exaggerated fashion—exactly what he thought and felt. In most cases, this was perfectly fine, but there were situations when maintaining a more neutral expression would have been desirable. For example, during a brainstorming session, he was obviously critical of certain ideas and more favorable toward others. And he could really get himself into trouble if he verbally supported an idea, but his nonverbal behavior suggested otherwise. Over time, Alex learned how to regulate his facial expressions and align them with his words, which reduced others' experience of mixed messages and led to more open discussions.

Gestures

Hand gestures are common in all cultures and an expedient means of communicating one's feelings and thoughts. Well-known examples include fingers in a "V" peace sign, crossed fingers for good luck, a thumbs-up, and a raised fist of victory. (Readers familiar with the Star Trek series will remember Spock's famous Vulcan live-long-and-prosper hand gesture.) Some cultures are very well known for utilizing gestures. For example, Italians are famous for talking with their hands. However, the meaning of a hand gesture can differ significantly from culture to culture. A notorious example is that of President Nixon who, on a visit to Brazil, enthusiastically greeted a waiting crowd with what Americans would recognize as an A-OK sign (touch forefinger to thumb and point the three remaining digits upward). Unfortunately, such a gesture in the Brazilian culture is akin to giving the middle finger in America. Obviously, it is quite important for those who work in multinational organizations to become educated in the meanings of gestures across cultures. While gestures may not play a large role in business communication and difficult conversations, we can imagine that a friendly gesture such as a thumbs-up or a wave hello or goodbye would be viewed in a positive and collaborative light.

Body Language and Posture

Like facial expressions, our body language supplements our words. How we position our bodies can reveal how we feel and what we think, but it can also mean nothing at all. We tend not to give a lot of thought to how we sit, stand, or position our arms, but other people may attribute significant meaning to what they believe our body language communicates, whether consciously or unconsciously. What does it mean when people slump in their chair? Does it mean they are tired or disinterested? Perhaps they are embarrassed and trying to avoid eye contact, or they lack self-confidence. Maybe doing so feels better on their bad back. Or it could just be that they have poor posture. Bouncing knees, tapping fingers, crossed arms and legs, hands on hips, hands clasped in front or behind, palms open or closed—each contributes to our interpretation of another's state of mind and has the potential to exacerbate or reduce conflict. While how we physically comport ourselves is largely unconscious, it can be helpful at times to be more intentional, especially during critical conversations.

You can use your body language to facilitate healthy conversations. Here are some tips for creating a sense of safety and openness:

► Keep your hands to yourself; do not touch the other person.

► Keep your hands by your side.

► Keep your arms and legs uncrossed.

► Avoid pointing your finger.

► Keep your palms open rather than fisted.

► Relax your shoulders.

► Keep your feet shoulder-width apart and pointed directly in front of you rather than spread wide and outward.

► Avoid quick, sudden movements.

► Avoid fidgeting and other expressions of energy, such as bouncing your knee or tapping your finger.

► Avoid leaning overly forward and crowding the other person's physical space.

Another type of body language is mirroring, which refers to imitating the nonverbal behavior of others; it is parroting without words. Most of the time this is done unconsciously. However, it is an excellent technique to make people feel comfortable with you and leads to a feeling of connectedness. It creates a sense of familiarity and can help defuse a particularly difficult conversation. So, if you are having a conversation with someone who crosses her arms or legs, you may want to do so as well. When talking with someone who speaks quickly, you may want to increase your cadence. You may also mirror a person's words, which is one reason that paraphrasing is so important in making people feel understood.

I once gave a workshop when, during a break, a participant approached me and said angrily, "I cannot believe I have to waste an entire afternoon listening to a talk about respect!" (Fortunately, I was forewarned that she was the reason for the class.) As I began to respond, she immediately cut me off and said, "You don't even know what to say, do you? In fact, you are so defensive, you have your arms crossed!" To which I replied, "Actually, I find the room quite chilly." After informing me that I was lying, she stormed off. One of the unfortunate realities is that such abrasive people instill fear in those around them, so that others are afraid to speak up, especially when that person is a department manager, as she was.

I want to encourage you to become self-aware of your body language and posture and how it might be interpreted by others, especially during an emotionally intense conversation. Imagine viewing yourself as an objective third party. In my experience, people can become more readily conscious of their body language than their facial expressions and thus are better able to make adjustments. I also suggest that you pay attention to others' body language and what unconscious thoughts and feelings it triggers in you. For example, when the other person crosses her arms, is your interpretation that she is becoming defensive or defiant? How does your assessment affect your feelings, thoughts, and actions?

Body language is certainly not innocuous. While few will take me up on this suggestion, record a video of yourself in a meeting or giving a presentation and review it with the sound turned off. (Several online meeting video platforms make this quite simple.) As you review the video, try to imagine that you are looking at somebody else. Does this person look engaged? Curious? Bored? Preoccupied? Anxious? Do any movements or expressions suggest conflict or aggression? Do these physical expressions match your internal thoughts and feelings at the time? After assessing your body language, consider if you might make any adjustments in how you come across. If you are unable to film yourself at work, even a homemade video with family and friends in a social setting can be instructive.

Physical Distance

Physical distance, also known as the study of proxemics, can dramatically escalate conflict. During an emotionally charged conversation, closeness suggests aggression and an attempt to dominate or overwhelm another person. An exaggerated but clear-cut example is that of boxers who go nose-to-nose during prefight press conferences. In contrast, when we are trying to avoid conflict or are preparing ourselves for flight, we will stand farther apart than our cultural norms—about four feet for Americans and two to three feet for Europeans. Sadly, due to COVID-19, we are all well aware that social distancing requires us to stand six feet apart. Of course, being physically close to another may also be indicative of friendship and feelings of affection.

Obviously, be very aware of encroaching on others' physical space. If you perceive someone is at all nervous or anxious, keep farther away than usual. Be sensitive to an individual who is trying to create more distance and be careful not to unconsciously step or lean forward to close the gap. It is important to know how to deal with situations in which someone is trying to use physical proximity for the purpose of intimidation. While the tactic of "standing your ground" is certainly an option, it may also intensify an already fraught situation. If you are standing, simply sitting down can diminish emotions because it creates separation and leads to a less rigid and more relaxed posture; hopefully, the other person will sit as well. You might have noticed that it is much easier to get animated and energized from a standing position. In fact, it is when we become excitable that we stand up.

If sitting down is not an option or does not have the desired effect, I suggest creating separation by simply stepping away. If you do and the person moves closer, say, "I ask that you respect my personal space and take a step back." If the person refuses to honor your request, then remove yourself from the situation by saying, "I am going to walk away now. Please respect my decision to do so." In any of these scenarios, do your best to keep your composure in order to limit the likelihood of further aggressive behavior.

Vocal Qualities

The vocal qualities of our speech, such as volume, cadence, pitch, and tone, all play a critical role in how we send and receive messages. This field of study is known as paralinguistics. When we modulate what we say, we inject emphasis and emotion, and influence how the listener hears and interprets our message. Of course, what we intend to communicate and how it is perceived by our listener may be quite different, especially during emotionally heightened conversations. For example, it would be easy to construe the words, "Yeah, right" as either accusatory or confirmatory. Or imagine saying, "I'm running out of options here," and your colleague responds, "Really." Did you hear, "Really." "Really?" or "Really!" Even expressed in the form of a question, the reply may come across as either sincere or sarcastic, and depending on our interpretation, our response would likely be dramatically different.

When it comes to how we say things, our emotions typically give us away. Obviously, this is only of concern under certain instances. When we are happy and excited, the pitch, cadence, and volume of our voice naturally increase. I have never won a lottery or even a raffle, but screaming seems completely fitting in such a situation. (Remember, context matters.) Screaming in a business environment, of course, is never appropriate. Human beings are quite good at recognizing an angry tone of voice, which makes sense from an evolutionary perspective. When we get angry, our volume and cadence typically increase. However, for some, it will produce the opposite effect. (When my father got particularly angry, he would speak more slowly and softly, but his tone made his emotion unequivocal.)

We have probably all raised our voices in anger and wished later that we had not done so. As humans, we very much want to stay in control of our emotions. Apologizing is always appropriate in such instances. It is perhaps the only, and unquestionably most efficient, way to get a relationship and conversation back on track. There are times when, based on someone's reaction, we realize that what we said did not come across as we had intended. For example, I may want to give a team member some constructive feedback on her presentation, but after I do so she says, "Why do you have to be so critical of everything I do?!" I intended my comments to be helpful, but they came across as belittling. To make matters worse, my knee-jerk response might increase tension—for example, "What is wrong with you? All I'm trying to do is help!" Communication can go from constructive to destructive in a hurry!

Written Word

While we may not have to worry about nonverbal communication issues with the written word, we continually infuse meaning into what we read, from a text message to the text of the Constitution. In general, the shorter the communication, the more prone we are to read into it, and to do so inaccurately (simple responses such as "yes" or "seven o'clock" aside). The less context we have, the more ambiguous the message. And, depending on our relationship history, we may very much misconstrue the intentions of the sender. Imagine your boss texting you, "What did you get done today?" Did this come across as accusatory, caring, or micromanaging? So many of our unconscious biases come into play when we try to decode even a simple message. Again, one of the most important tips that I can give you is if you find yourself thinking, *I wonder what she means by that*, ask her!

In addition to the actual words, punctuation matters a lot. "I love cooking my family and my cat" is way different than, "I love cooking, my family, and my cat." It is interesting to consider from a generational perspective the varied use of punctuation. For example, younger employees may view periods at the end of text messages as foreboding or a sign of anger, while older generations may view this simply as grammatically correct. (Many members of the younger generation view punctuation as optional!) How one begins (salutation) or signs off (valediction) on a correspondence can have an interesting impact on some people. For example, I have a European colleague who finds the lack of a formal salutation and valediction quite rude. Personally, I feel that both should be included in professional correspondences. Is it too much to write (not automate), "Regards, Paul"?

Underlining, italicizing, boldfacing, highlighting, and capitalizing words create all kinds of emotion, especially in brief communications such as text messages. Quite frankly, I find emphasizing words in this way largely unnecessary, often irritating, and at times responsible for increasing conflict way more than resolving it. (I am not even going to touch on emojis.) Despite my aversion to stating the painfully obvious, DO NOT HAVE EMOTIONALLY CHARGED CONVERSATIONS OVER EMAIL OR TEXT!!! In the spirit of promoting healthy written conversations, use correct grammar and punctuation, provide context, be concise, and use simple, clear, and straightforward language.

SUMMARY

Are you feeling self-conscious after reading this chapter? After I wrote it, I could not have a discussion without imagining how I came across to others. I did not even want to look in the mirror! Given that your expressions, posture, and distance from others contribute to escalating or defusing conflict situations, becoming aware of your nonverbal behavior is clearly important. Whenever you are in an emotionally fraught situation, the most important thing you can do is remain calm and composed—both verbally and nonverbally. Do not say or do anything that would indicate your upset or potentially serve to rile up the other person. Also, in general, make sure that your verbal and nonverbal communication align with one another.

UP NEXT

In the next chapter we will take a look at specific words, phrases, and expressions that can lead to confrontation or turn an intense conversation into a collaborative one.

ON YOUR PLAYING FIELD

1. Think about your last heated conversation. How did you respond in terms of your nonverbal communication? Do you think it helped to quell the exchange or intensify it? How could you have acted differently?
2. How should you deal with situations in which another person's nonverbal cues are triggering you and causing an escalation?
3. Prior to a particularly difficult conversation, consider practicing in the mirror and pay particular attention to how your nonverbal communication might be interpreted by the other.
4. Ask a colleague who was present during a tense conversation for feedback about your body language and tone of voice. Did you remain composed and professional?

CHAPTER 7

LOADED LANGUAGE

Loaded language refers to words, phrases, statements, and questions that evoke strong emotions. As discussed previously, there are a litany of factors that moderate our interpretation of language and influence how we respond to others, including our vocal tone, body language, context, and unconscious biases, as well as our motivations, state of mind, and mood. The more cognizant we are of these influences, the better we can control our emotions and respond in a calm, intentional, and measured fashion.

Let us focus our attention on the spoken word. To state the obvious, a conversation is a dialogue between two or more people, and dialogue is composed of words—including those communicated by sign language. A conversation without words is simply a staring contest. Some words and expressions induce joy or calm, while others trigger us; that is, they cause a negative spike in our emotions and have us "seeing red." The following list of statements and rhetorical questions often serve to further escalate emotional conversations. In general, they come across as disrespectful, critical, belittling, dictatorial, threatening, dismissive, untruthful, or an attack on one's character. In short, they make healthy conversations impossible. As you read over the list, identify which serve as your personal push buttons:

► Are you being serious?

► Are you done yet?

► Are you sure you want to go down that road?

► Do you actually believe what you're saying?

► Get over it already!

► Honestly, this is not that hard to understand.

► How many times do I have to explain this to you before you're going to get it?

► I wouldn't expect you to understand.

► If I wanted your opinion, I would have asked for it.

► It is what it is.

► It might be a problem for you, but it isn't for me.

► Now you're just talking nonsense.

► Once again, it's all about you!

► Stop being so dramatic!

► Stop being so stubborn!

► Take it or leave it.

► That simply isn't true.

► This doesn't concern you.

► This isn't going to end well for you.

► What is it about "No" that you don't understand?

► What you're talking about just isn't relevant.

► What, exactly, is your problem?

► Why are you becoming so defensive?

- ► Why are you making this such a big deal?

- ► You can't be serious!

- ► You have no idea what you're talking about.

- ► You need to change your attitude right now!

- ► You need to come to your senses and start living in reality.

- ► You need to stop talking and start listening.

- ► You wouldn't understand.

- ► You're being overly sensitive.

- ► You're getting upset over nothing.

- ► You're just confused.

- ► You're letting your emotions get the best of you.

- ► You're lying.

- ► You're out of control.

- ► You're wrong.

Which of these phrases makes you see red? Are you guilty of using them? Can you think of other expressions that belong on this list? How do you react when confronted with such inflammatory questions and statements? Unfortunately, our first instinct is usually to verbally retaliate without considering the impact of doing so. For example, if confronted with "What's your problem?" an automatic response may be, "*You're* my problem!" Or a ready rejoinder to "You can't be a serious" is "Oh, I'm very serious." And a quick reply to "Are you sure that you want to go down that road?" may be "I can't wait." Such exchanges clearly exacerbate conflict and promote confrontation; there is absolutely no chance of collaboration once verbal sparring begins. And if you really want to escalate the situation and risk doing permanent damage to the relationship, make the argument public via email, text chains, or social media.

When it comes to verbal exchanges, as a general rule, you want to avoid any "You" statements. Focus on "I" statements to communicate and take responsibility for your thoughts, feelings, and emotions. "You" statements often feel like an attack and are likely to make the other party defensive, especially when combined with the words "need to," or "must," which sound like commands. Faced with "You must do *x*," a person's automatic thought is *I don't have to do anything, and certainly not what you tell me to do!* Other words to avoid are "always" and "never," as such extremes are easily debunked. For example, "You never tell the truth" or "You are always out for yourself." Also, while it may not have you see red, it is best to avoid the word "but" as it tends to negate whatever the other person just said. For example, "I believe you, but . . ."

De-escalating Language

Obviously, there are also expressions that help to de-escalate situations, restore civil dialogue, and increase collaboration. In general, any phrase that communicates empathy, a genuine and sincere apology, or a sense of ownership for causing or contributing to the conflict helps calm emotional waters. Useful phrases include:

- ► I am sorry for having jumped to conclusions before hearing your side of the story and getting all the facts.

- ► I am sorry that I let my emotions get the best of me.

- ► I apologize.

- ► I can see that I had a clear role to play in all this.

- ► I never thought about it from your perspective.

- ► I promise to be more thoughtful in the future.

- ► I should have given you the benefit of the doubt.

- ► I should have taken more time to ask you questions instead of making assumptions.

- ► I was mistaken.

- ► In retrospect, it was wrong of me to blame you. I should have taken more responsibility for what happened.

- ► What I said (or did) was inconsiderate, and I apologize.

- ► What I said was inappropriate.

- ► You're right.

How do you respond when others use this sort of language with you? Can you feel your blood pressure decrease and shoulders relax? Does it allow you to listen more fully to the other person? It is remarkable how a few simple words can completely change the course of a conversation. No matter how mad you are, it is hard to keep yelling at someone after they say, "I want to apologize to you." I encourage you to try it the next time you find yourself in an argument. If nothing else, apologize for raising your voice and not fully listening to the other person, or perhaps for being stubborn. Are there other phrases you can think of that can reduce negative emotions?

There is one phrase I find quite interesting, as it has the potential to increase, decrease, or have no impact on another's emotional state: "Well, we will just have to agree to disagree." I am not a proponent of this statement because it tends to prematurely stop the discussion and, thus, compromise any potential collaboration. I find this statement to be an easy out and an excuse for not working sincerely to resolve an issue. People say this when they have little interest in seeking to understand the other person's perspective or find common ground. Healthy conversations require an authentic desire to work together, not just pay lip service to the idea.

A useful response to the agree-to-disagree line may be something like, "While I will respect your decision to leave it at that, I would very much appreciate spending a few minutes trying to identify areas that we can agree on. I think we owe it to our client and colleagues to do whatever we can to reach agreement and make progress on this matter." Perhaps offer to continue the conversation the next day to give you both a chance to think things over. Such an approach is likely to keep the discussion going and dramatically improve the chances of resolving the issue.

The Silent Treatment

Have you ever received the silent treatment from someone you care about? Is there anything worse? I am not talking about when we take a break from a conversation to cool off; rather, when someone simply refuses to have any interaction with you at all. In these cases, no language or discourse is occurring; the silence says it all. In a work setting, such behavior is obviously wholly unprofessional and inappropriate. Yet I have seen it, and you probably have as well.

Sometimes these stretches last a few hours or days, sometimes forever. As we have discussed, the adverse impact of conflict extends far beyond the two people who are in it. If you ever find yourself in such a situation, my best advice is to say directly and sincerely, "Let's talk about it." You must be 100 percent committed to making the relationship work. While you should be respectful and allow the other person time and space, you also need to be persistent in extending the proverbial olive branch. Again, if not for yourself, then for others. Obviously, if you are the one giving the silent treatment, get over it. Your job is to do the best you can for your company and clients, and you cannot do that when you are not talking with your colleague.

SUMMARY

When you consider both verbal and nonverbal communication combined, it gives you an appreciation for how complex our interactions are with others—and how much can go wrong! Effective communicators are very intentional in what they say and how they say it, particularly when it comes to difficult conversations. Always do your best to keep your composure, regardless of what another person says to you. We all know the expression: "He is just trying to get a rise out of you." My advice is to rise above the situation and continue to be respectful and responsible for your communication. Remember, while a time-out is generally a good strategy, the silent treatment is not. *Saying nothing gets you nowhere.*

UP NEXT

In the next chapter, we will discuss the key strategies to use when you start to feel your emotional buttons being pushed. For now, think deeply about how language affects you personally and how you may have used it in the past to fuel rather than defuse tension, and what you can say to decrease conflict and foster collaboration.

ON YOUR PLAYING FIELD

1. What do people say to you during an argument that instantly triggers you?
2. How do you typically handle such situations, and how might you deal with them more productively?
3. What inflammatory comments do you make when you are angry and frustrated with others? What more appropriate language might you use?
4. Is there someone to whom you should apologize for your recent behavior?
5. If there is anyone with whom you are not currently speaking, fix it.

CHAPTER 8

PUSH-BUTTON MANAGEMENT

We all have push buttons—words and actions that trigger strong negative emotions. You may have recognized some of your own in the last chapter. In fact, sometimes all it takes is seeing a particular person's name on an email or a text to trigger these emotions, without having even read it! General examples of push buttons include being lied to or taken advantage of, someone turning and walking away during a conversation, being criticized, having your character questioned, having information withheld from you, having someone take credit for your work, or being told you are unqualified for an assignment. When confronted with such situations, you likely react without much thought, including any consideration for the consequences of your actions. In fact, a common experience in these situations is feeling out of control. This chapter will teach you specific cognitive and behavioral strategies that will help you maintain your composure during contentious interactions.

Identifying Your Personal Push Buttons

As with unconscious biases, the first step in dealing with push buttons is to identify them. Once identified, you can recognize them in real time and say to yourself, "Wait. This is a push button for me, and I know how to deal with it." As a rough analogy, imagine driving your car and suddenly coming upon a patch of black ice. While you may not be able to avoid it, you can use the skills you have developed to negotiate it effectively. The same is true when faced with "icy" interpersonal circumstances. Take a moment and think about some of the things people say or do that cause you to see red. In the spaces that follow, write down examples of your own push buttons and the feelings associated with them. An example is provided.

TRIGGER	ASSOCIATED FEELING(S)
EXAMPLE:	
When someone talks behind my back	Disrespected, angry
1.	
2.	
3.	
4.	
5.	

As you look over this list, do you notice a common theme? Where you have listed your feelings, how often did the word "disrespected" show up? For many, feeling disrespected is a major push button. Mutual respect is necessary for relationships to work, however you define or measure it. In my first book, *Carrots and Sticks Don't Work*, I presented the thesis that respect drives employee engagement. I could hardly have imagined that the book would end up being translated into numerous languages, sold around the world, and appear on multiple lists as one of the most important human resource books of all time. Its success is a testament to the power of respect, and while the definition of respect and its behavioral manifestations vary from culture to culture, there is no doubt of its importance to all people. In the words of the great Jackie Robinson: "I'm not concerned with your liking or disliking me. All I ask is that you respect me as a human being." Because disrespect is such a significant trigger and contributing factor to escalating conflict, I want to dive a little deeper into the significance of respect in our lives.

Why Respect Matters

Respect is related to survival. To gain some perspective on this thesis, let's take a look at various historical examples of respect. Consider the following: until the late 1800s, it was perfectly acceptable to challenge a rival to a duel, typically to defend one's honor after feeling disrespected. As many of us know, one of the most notorious duels was between Aaron Burr and Alexander Hamilton. While the two men had a history of political rivalry, the literal triggering event was a derogatory comment Hamilton reportedly made toward Burr at a dinner party, which was subsequently reported in a local newspaper. As a result of this assault on his character and Hamilton's unwillingness to make amends, Burr challenged Hamilton to a duel that occurred on July 11, 1804, on a cliff in Weehawken, New Jersey. Hamilton was mortally wounded at the same site where his eldest son, Philip, was killed in a duel three years prior. These incredibly erudite and accomplished men were willing to kill or be killed over an issue of public disrespect. Can you imagine if social media had been around 200 years ago?!

Gang members kill one another explicitly over the issue of respect. Their currency includes their colors, turf, and reputation. In this culture, if you get "dissed" (disrespected), you have no choice but to challenge the other to a "duel." And of course, prison inmates will confront one another in order to gain respect. Consider the following quote given during an interview with convicted felon Oluwasegun Akinsanya: "The other prisoners mostly left me alone, because my charge, second-degree murder, gave me a certain amount of respect."* To allow oneself to be disrespected would be considered weak, which equates to being vulnerable.

On a larger scale, respect for human rights often plays a role in revolutions and wars, including the American Revolution, Civil War, and more recently the Velvet Revolution in 1989, during which Czechoslovakia extricated itself from the oppression of communist rule. A pointed geopolitical example is that of the nuclear arms reduction talks between the United States and Iran in 2018. In the words of Mohammad Javad Zarif, the Iranian minister of foreign affairs, "Mutual trust is not a requirement to start negotiations— mutual respect is a requirement."†

The relationship between respect and life and death can also be viewed, unfortunately, in the context of one taking his or her own life. Throughout Japan's history, suicide has been viewed as a means for restoring honor or respect by atoning for wrongdoing. When defeated in battle, samurai would often commit suicide to preserve their honor. Even more extreme is the concept of "honor killings," in which a person may feel it his responsibility to kill a family member who has brought dishonor upon the family. In other cultures, including that of

---

* S. Akinsanya, "A History of Violence," Toronto Life, January 21, 2016, https://torontolife .com/city/life/my-life-in-street-gangs/.
† K. Hjelmgaard, "Iran Open to Talks with US if Trump Changes Approach to Nuclear Deal, Top Diplomat Says," *USA Today*, November 15, 2017, https://www.usatoday.com /story/news/world/2018/11/05/iran-united-states-president-donald-trump-nuclear -deal-foreign-minister-mohammad-javad-zarif/1859375002/.

the United States, one might view suicide as the ultimate form of self-loathing and self-disrespect. Whether it is on the individual, gang, national, or global level, respect is a matter of life and death.

Let's get back to the workplace. Why do you think it matters so much to be respected by your colleagues? It matters because when we are respected we are viewed as having value, which translates into security. People whose contributions are valued tend to get promoted, not fired. Respect also equates to influence and power. If you think about the people you respect the most, you will likely also find that they have had the greatest influence on you and, typically, vice versa. The more respected we are at work, the more likely we are to be put into leadership positions and the greater influence we will exert on the organization and others.

The highly undesirable experience of being disrespected can arise from a number of situations, such as when we feel excluded from conversations and passed over for promotions, or when we feel information is being withheld, our contributions are being minimized, we are being taken advantage of, and/or our opinions ignored. In these circumstances, we become unsure and insecure about our position and place within our organization. Words and actions that we interpret as disrespectful and devaluing make us feel vulnerable and activate our sympathetic nervous system. In survival mode, we are more likely to aggressively defend our positions and seek to prove others wrong. And while collaboration might be the goal, we enter into a mindset that paints others as opponents and leads us to gear up for confrontation instead. *In such a mindset, if the other person were to extend an olive branch, it would just look like a stick.*

By the way, did you ever notice that the same people (or person) and same issues get us stirred up time and again? We know who and what triggers us, yet we persist in allowing ourselves to get angry and upset. The same story plays itself out with the same ending, just like Charlie Brown running at the football and Lucy pulling it away—every time. Charlie Brown gets mad at Lucy for doing what she always does. Will we ever learn?

My good friend John's work nemesis is Fiona. As with any good friend, he calls me when he needs to blow off steam. "Paul, let me tell you what Fiona did today. . . . Can you freaking believe it?" While I would normally just listen and commiserate, one day I responded, "Actually, yes. It seems that Fiona has been doing some version of that for years. What I can't understand is why it seems to keep surprising and bothering you so much." Though it has taken him a while, when issues now arise, he thinks to himself, "Fiona is just being Fiona. How else would she act?" Do you have a Fiona in your life? As we will discuss in the next chapter, with effort and intention, you will be able to alter your mindset and how you think about and respond to others.

Owning Your Emotions and Reactions

When someone pushes your buttons, how do you usually react? Do you tend to get defensive, passive-aggressive, or even aggressive? Do you raise your voice, embarrass the person on an email chain, "forget" to include her on a meeting invite, gossip, withhold information, or, worse, provide misleading information? Do you take the time to fully consider the impact of your reactions, including how others might view you in light of them? Your automatic response can reflect poorly on you, especially when your reaction is overt and public, such as speaking negatively about the person with colleagues.

Have you ever said or done anything that you regretted? I know I have. In almost all cases, my thoughtless reaction exacerbated the tension. The more aware we are of our triggers, the more capable we are of controlling our emotions and reactions when confronted with them, and the less likely we are to say and do things that escalate conflict. Life is a lot easier when you can control your emotions independently of what others do or say. As my motorcycle-riding buddy Jack likes to say, you get to be "unmessable."

Words only hurt if you let them. As the famous saying goes, "Sticks and stones may break my bones, but words will never hurt me." Whether you experience another's words or actions as hurtful is entirely up to you. This is extremely important to understand and fully accept. No one can *make* you feel any way. To say that your boss made you angry or upset is disempowering, disingenuous, and a ploy to avoid taking responsibility for your feelings. Giving away your personal power by assigning blame and responsibility to someone for how you feel is also a good way to escalate conflict. For example, as much as we may be tempted to tell someone, "You're driving me crazy!" do not do it, or you may get the response, "No, *you're* driving yourself crazy because you know I'm right." When it comes to quelling your emotions, the place to start is by taking full responsibility for them—whether you want to or not. If you fully own your feelings, then you control how you react to others regardless of what they say or do. This realization that you get to govern your emotions independent of others should leave you feeling inspired and empowered. Commit to taking responsibility for your emotions and actions in all situations.

People say they are committed to all kinds of things, like being healthier and more organized, saving money, and not procrastinating. In reality, we are committed to what we actually do and have in our lives. If you say that you are committed to quitting smoking and you keep smoking, well, then you are really committed to smoking. If you say that you are committed to not procrastinating but continue to leave important tasks until the last minute, you are clearly committed to procrastination. If you say that you are committed to having a collaborative relationship with a coworker but you continue to argue and speak poorly about her to others, you are actually committed to having an unprofessional and unhealthy relationship. *Here is the deal: you get to declare commitment when your actions reliably align with your intentions.* For example, you are committed to being a person of integrity when you are honest and keep your word at all times under all circumstances. You do not get to pick and choose when you feel like acting with integrity. You are either in or out.

So, are you committed to taking 100 percent responsibility for your emotions, no matter what others say and do? Or do you choose to give your power away and let other people push your buttons? If so, then feel free to react however you like during disagreements with coworkers—be as unprofessional as you want. And why not? You get to blame the other person for your inappropriate words and actions instead of holding yourself accountable. Go ahead, use some of that push-button language we talked about in the previous chapter and fuel the conflict. Because, after all, that is the only way to respond to such a stubborn and egocentric colleague! The reality is that you get to choose how you respond in any situation. You are not some puppet attached to strings that others get to manipulate. Do not say that someone "yanks your chain," when doing so is simply not possible as a matter of reality.

If you choose to be committed to owning your thoughts and feelings and how you respond to others, then you need to make sure that your behavior is in alignment. This means that when someone says, "Do you even know what you're talking about?" or denigrates you behind your back, or constantly cuts you off in meetings, or any number of other comments or actions that normally have you seeing red, that you breathe deeply and respond professionally. It does not mean that you allow others to continue their bad behavior without addressing it. It means that you will handle the situation in a manner that honors your commitment and promotes a healthy relationship, not continued conflict. If a colleague begins to raise his voice or criticize your ideas, instead of getting upset and retaliating, respond in a calm, respectful, and straightforward manner.

When trying to change behavior, especially in the maelstrom of strong emotions, it is important to develop a prompt, at least initially. It can be as simple as writing, "I am committed to taking full responsibility for my thoughts, emotions, and reactions" on a sticky note. I suggest posting it on your mirror or refrigerator and reading it each morning. Also, reference your prompt before you have what you fear might be an untoward conversation or interaction with a colleague who has traditionally caused you angst. To increase your accountability, share your pledge with a trusted friend or colleague and ask her to bring it to your attention when you are acting otherwise.

If you really want to make a difference, speak to the person with whom you tend to have the most tension and say something along the lines of, "I know in the past I have tended to argue with you and become upset when we disagree. I want to apologize for acting that way and to let you know I am committed to remaining calm and fully professional whenever we speak. I would like to ask that if you feel I am acting otherwise you bring it to my attention." Or you might choose to say, "I want to acknowledge and apologize for not always having fully listened to your perspective in the past. I am committing to doing so going forward, and if you don't feel that I am, please tell me." What might be the impact on a coworker if you said such things? What would be the impact on you? In a matter of seconds, you can completely change the narrative of a relationship. It really is that simple. This is incredibly empowering and obviates feeling like you are at the mercy of another's actions.

Meditation: Calming the Chatter

I imagine you are familiar with the idea of losing your breath. This typically happens under extreme emotional conditions—both good and bad—such as a surprise marriage proposal (which I made during the writing of this book) or a near car accident. Although typically not as extreme as these examples, when any type of conflict arises, our sympathetic nervous system kicks in and triggers a cascade of stress hormones. This in turn leads to physiological responses such as shallow and rapid breathing, dilated pupils, and an increase in heart rate and blood pressure. With our body in survival mode, we react instinctively and without rational consideration of the facts, circumstances, options, or impact of our actions.

When you get triggered, it may feel like an emotional wave washing over you. However, unlike when you are in the ocean, do not hold your breath! One of the best and most powerful ways we can calm our minds and limit the activation of our sympathetic nervous system is through controlled breathing. As you may well know, the practice of meditation has a host of psychological, emotional, and physical benefits, including a reduction in stress and anxiety. There are several different forms of meditation, including transcendental, visualization, and mindfulness, that I will review at a very high level and encourage you to learn more about, should you find them beneficial. These techniques can be instrumental in helping to increase your sense of calm and decrease the likelihood that your sympathetic nervous system will activate when you feel emotionally triggered. (For the record, I practice meditation but am no practitioner. If you are interested in learning more, a good place to start is with the work of Jon Kabat-Zinn.)

Transcendental Meditation

Transcendental meditation, also known as TM, was developed by the Indian guru Maharishi Mahesh Yogi in the 1950s. This type of meditation involves the use of a mantra and is typically practiced twice daily for 20 minutes in a seated position with eyes closed. Mantras can be sounds, words, phrases, or even a poem or saying, such as the Lord's Prayer. In very general terms, whatever mantra you choose should resonate with you in a positive, peaceful, and life-affirming way. Put simply, it should make you feel good. During the 20-minute practice, the mantra is repeated over and over again while breathing in deeply. Typically, the mantra is said silently, however, it can also be verbalized and even chanted. Each syllable and word can be accentuated to increase focus and attention. Let's give it a try:

1. Identify a mantra that might work for you. There are lots of examples online. If you do not know where to begin, try a very simple one such as, "I am calm."

2. Find a quiet, peaceful place as free from distraction as possible.

3. Sit comfortably with your back straight and shoulders relaxed.

4. Gently close your eyes.

5. Set an intention, for example, to calm your mind or generate self-compassion.

6. Begin breathing slowly and deeply in and out through your nose. Remain focused on your breath and the sensation of air entering your body and filling your lungs.

7. Fully exhale and allow the air to leave your body. Exert no effort. Seek to be fully and solely present to the experience and sensations. As extraneous thoughts enter your mind, merely acknowledge their existence, and gently return to a focus on your breath. Do not judge yourself. Do not allow yourself to think that you are "good" or "bad" at this practice; you are neither. You just are.

8. Breathe deeply and gently for a few minutes, and when you feel a sense of relaxation and calmness, introduce the mantra during your inhale. Take the time that you need; you should not feel rushed or pressured in any way. Consider that you have taken millions of breaths without effort throughout your life.

9. In total, practice this exercise for 20 minutes. If this seems too long for you, start with five minutes, and work your way toward longer periods of time. So that you do not have to worry about keeping track of the minutes, you may want to set a timer on your phone. If you are able, make the alarm a gentle sound, such as chimes or chirping birds. Obviously, put your phone on silent and keep it out of sight during the meditation.

10. When you have finished, slowly open your eyes and remain seated and calm for another minute or two before rising. Complete this exercise two to three times a day, including prior to engaging in what you believe will be a stressful interaction.

Visualization

The general practice of visualization is extremely well studied and effective in enhancing performance across many situations. As the name might suggest, this practice involves visualizing success under various conditions and is used by many professional athletes. For example, Olympic skier and gold medalist Lindsey Vonn said that by the time she gets to the gate to begin a race, she has already run it 100 times in her head, including the breathing patterns she will use and how she will shift her weight during the race.[*]

In the workplace, you might use visualization in preparation for an important presentation by vividly imagining walking into the conference room, confidently going through the presentation, effectively answering questions, and then receiving praise from participants after the meeting. Obviously, like Vonn, you would practice being successful by playing this scenario out many times in your mind.

In terms of applying visualization to difficult conversations, imagine going through the whole interaction from first word to last. Throughout, use deep breathing to help you remain calm and focused. In addition to using this form of meditation on future experiences, I also find it helpful to visualize past experiences in which I may have become emotionally triggered and did not handle myself as I wish I had. I rework these experiences in my mind until I imagine having been calm during them. I find that if I do so over and over, I can remove the sting of that memory, feel better about the experience, and be more prepared for similar situations moving forward.

Mindfulness

While visualization and transcendental meditation are quite planned, mindfulness can be practiced at any time, under any

---

[*] Anna Williams, "8 Successful People Who Use the Power of Visualization," mbgmindfulness, March 2020, https://www.mindbodygreen.com/0-20630/8-successful-people -who-use-the-power-of-visualization.html.

circumstance. Put simply, it is the act of bringing your attention to the present moment and doing so from an emotionless, detached perspective. It is as though you are a spectator simply viewing a scene without judgment. For example, imagine being berated by your manager and instead of becoming angry and upset, simply observe what is happening; notice that you are standing in place while looking at your boss who is speaking in a raised voice. He is blaming you for losing a deal because you did not follow up promptly with a potential client. You continue to breathe deeply and remain calm, refraining from making judgments about yourself, your boss, or the situation. When practicing mindfulness in such a situation, you are better able to think clearly and strategically and respond in a manner that will likely decrease the other's agitated state. As with visualization, reenact this and similar scenarios over and over in your head. Consider that you are preparing for your own Olympic sport.

Decrease Your Stress

There are a variety of visual prompts that may help you remain calm under stressful circumstances. Pictures of loved ones, including pets, remind us of what is truly important and help keep situations in perspective. Memories of happy occasions and fun events, such as a vacation or playing softball with friends do the same. Quite frankly, anything that makes you smile is helpful. Aside from visual reminders, there are a whole host of other activities that can decrease your stress levels. Some people listen to calming music. Physical activity is another popular de-stressor; simply taking a walk outside can be extremely beneficial. Other potential ways to decrease stress include cooking, gardening, watching your favorite TV show or movie, playing with a pet, talking to a friend or family member, making art or crafting, journaling, or taking a nap. Perhaps there is a physical object that helps to ground you, such as a memento or keepsake from a loved one. Anything that helps you to relax, feel safe, and think clearly can make all the difference when you are faced with stressful conversations or situations. Find and write down the things that calm you. More importantly, do them!

Know When to Gain Time and Distance

The most critical first step when confronted with an emotionally charged situation is, if possible, to physically remove yourself from it. Take a time-out. My father served in the Air Force as a flight instructor. He taught young pilots that when something goes wrong, the first thing to do is to sit on your hands—not start pulling levers or pushing buttons. Rather, calm yourself, assess the situation, and consider your options.

Whenever you feel particularly triggered, especially when caught off guard, your best strategy is simply to remove yourself from the individual and situation. The physical distance need not be great; closing (not slamming) your office door may do the trick. Of course, turning off the video and "hanging up" during a conference call are easy solutions. Depending on the circumstances, the time-out may be entirely in your own head and last only a few seconds, or it may require several minutes or hours without interaction with the other person. (Longer than a day or two and you are practicing the silent treatment.) Not only does such a time-out give you the opportunity to calm down and plan the most constructive way to reengage with the person, but it also allows the other to do the same.

At times, when you are suddenly approached by a colleague who begins a conversation for which you are unprepared, it may be awkward or difficult to get that needed space. Here are a few simple phrases that may help you "get away":

1. I'd really like to talk about this, but I'm running late to another meeting.

2. Obviously, this is important for us to discuss. When is good for you tomorrow?

3. I'm really glad that you brought this up. Let me check my calendar and send you a meeting invite.

4. Clearly, this is important for us to talk about. I'm just in the middle of something, and I want to make sure to give this matter the attention it deserves. How about we get together this afternoon when I can focus more clearly?

5. Wow, this is news to me. I'm going to need some more information before I can give you an answer.

6. Our colleague Sue needs to be brought into this conversation. Let me reach out to her and get back to you.

If the request to speak comes via email or text, do not feel compelled to respond immediately. In fact, if you feel compelled to do so, it is probably a good indication that you should wait!

SUMMARY

Healthy and productive conversations rely on us maintaining our cool. We all have emotional triggers; people are going to say and do things that increase our blood pressure. That is just the way it is. At the same time, we are not predetermined to experience upset and react with anger. You get to choose how you respond and who you are in the face of any situation with anyone. Regardless of how the conversation actually goes, keeping your composure in the face of emotional triggers may be an enormous victory over the past for you.

UP NEXT

When facing a difficult conversation, what is your mindset? Do you still dread the thought, or are you beginning to see it as an opportunity to build a more collaborative relationship? The mindset that you have going into and during a difficult conversation is critical to the outcome. Read the next chapter with an open mind!

ON YOUR PLAYING FIELD

1. What specifically makes you feel disrespected? How do you respond? What might you say to yourself in those moments that would prevent you from becoming triggered?

2. Do you have a Fiona in your life? Someone who always seems to trigger you? What would it take for you not to react reflexively? How might you respond differently in the future?

3. Are there any areas of your life in which you say that you are committed but your actions tell a different story? If so, are you willing to fully commit? If yes, what will you do differently to bring your behavior in line with your word and ensure success?

4. You do not know if a strategy is going to be effective unless you give it a shot. If you have not tried meditation before, now is the time! Think about an experience in your past in which you let your emotions get the best of you. Then use breathing and visualization to imagine how you would choose to manage the situation now. Or take on a current issue and use meditation and visualization to set yourself and the other person up for a healthy conversation. Remember, in order to be successful, you must practice your visualizations many times.

CHAPTER 9

ENGAGING MINDSET

Our attitude about an upcoming event significantly impacts our experience of it. Have you ever had a significant other drag you to a social gathering with the promise of having a good time when you absolutely know that you will hate it? How often did you end up being surprised by how much you enjoyed yourself? Probably not often. If we say that we are going to be miserable, then we are going to be miserable, even, sadly, if only to prove the other person wrong. When we believe something will go a certain way, then we act in ways that fulfill that prophecy. Similarly, how well a difficult conversation goes is largely driven by the mindset we have going into it. This chapter provides advice on how to maintain an open and engaging mindset heading into emotionally charged conversations.

Shifting to an engaging mindset requires you to rework your attitude and approach toward what you believe are challenging conversations. Just as with cognitive biases, you may not be aware of how your current attitudes may be promoting conflict over collaboration. The good news is that you have complete control over your mindset and can begin making changes today that will positively impact any conversation. Realize that it will take time and practice to make enduring changes to your default ways of thinking, but those changes will pay dividends for the rest of your life. As you read the following tips, think of opportunities to apply each to current situations and specific people in your life.

Choose a Mindset of Collaboration over Confrontation

Perhaps the single biggest reason that conversations do not go well is because we believe they will not. When I know that I must have a conversation with someone I do not like about an issue that we passionately disagree on, let's be honest, my first thought is not a positive one. The truth is, I dread it. When we go into a situation expecting the worst, that is how it usually goes. We doom conversations and interactions before they even begin with our negative mindset, which triggers all kinds of anti-collaborative thoughts and behaviors, as well as predictions about how the other person is going to act. When heading into unfriendly conversations, recognize your default mindset and go about changing it. Give up those automatic thoughts, and picture you and the other person having a calm, open-minded, collaborative discussion. In other words, set a clear intention to have a healthy conversation. When you do this, you will show up as a very different person—and the other person will know it.

Own 100 Percent of the Conversation

In life, we usually assume 50 percent responsibility for how relationships go, and by extrapolation, we take 50 percent responsibility for our conversations. This mindset makes it quite easy to blame the other person when things do not go well. We say to ourselves, "I did my part. I can't help it if he didn't want to work together." What if you took 100 percent responsibility for a conversation—from initiating it, to how it goes, to how it ends? What if you were unconditionally committed to having a difficult conversation go well, regardless of the other person's words and actions? Does that sound empowering to you? It should.

Do you think the outcome will be more favorable? It will be. Do not let yourself off the hook by putting the other person on it.

Gain Perspective

In the children's story *Chicken Little*, the main character spreads unnecessary panic because she mistakes a falling acorn for the sky falling. In general, putting situations in perspective is important; when it comes to difficult conversations, it is especially critical. Think back to a situation that, at the time, caused catastrophic thinking and significant distress. When I reflect on my own, I remember feeling as though the sky was falling and the world was going to end. In retrospect, I wish that I had realized that while I may have had every right to be upset by the situation, I overreacted and caused myself and often others a good deal of anxiety. When issues arise that require a difficult conversation, think back to similar situations and remind yourself that you got through them just fine. In fact, you may find that previous experiences were even more challenging than the one you are currently facing. Most importantly, put the matter in perspective by focusing on what truly matters, namely, the health and well-being of you and your loved ones.

Eliminate Right Versus Wrong Thinking

During arguments, we often have the mindset that there can only be one "winner." This is known as zero-sum thinking. Thus, we desperately seek to make the other person wrong so we can be right, which naturally causes tension and fuels conflict. In reality, who is "right" and who is "wrong" is entirely subjective and situational. Both parties could be right, neither could be right, or both could be partially right. More problematic is how to judge right and wrong in the first place. Each party typically defines "right" in terms of what is in her best interest. And this evaluation is made based on the set of facts and circumstances known to the individual at that point in time, which, of course, can change. For example, a salesperson may want to push a high-margin product, but at the present, securing the necessary raw materials to make it may be difficult and expensive; in contrast, the plant manager may have a large surplus of a particular SKU and want to reduce that inventory. One decision is right from a sales perspective and the other from a plant perspective. However, factors such as market demands, shipping, raw material availability, costs, and product diversity goals may well change, which may affect the perspective of both sides. There are seldom entirely right decisions for every stakeholder in all situations. In the end, the mindset should not be who is right and who is wrong, but what is in the best interest of the overall organization and customer.

Stay Present

I do not know about you, but I constantly find my mind wandering and pulled in all sorts of directions. When it comes to increasing your attentiveness during a critical conversation, begin by eliminating the obvious distractions, namely turning off your phone and refraining from checking your email. If you have experienced being on the other side of such behavior, you know how disrespectful it feels. Personally, in order to limit distractions, I do not check my email, text messages, or voice mail within 15 minutes of any important meeting. Why? Because I am very aware that I could get a personal or professional message that would consume my thinking, but about which there is nothing I can do in the moment.

When you do find yourself distracted before going into a critical conversation, try to compartmentalize your thoughts and tell yourself that you will deal with the issue afterward. One trick I use is to schedule time on my calendar to do just that. It may sound silly, but it actually works quite well. I also use the technique of "clearing." The idea is as it sounds: clear your mind so that you may be more present by simply sharing your troubling thoughts with a colleague or friend.

After doing so, you may find it easier to compartmentalize the issue and focus more fully on the impending conversation. As discussed in the prior chapter, practicing mindfulness is a great way to keep yourself present.

Listen Without a Preconceived Bias

As discussed previously, our history with people creates filters through which we listen. If a peer is always critical of your work, then your bias might be to hear (or read) anything she says as derogatory. If people have been difficult in the past, then your expectation is likely that they will be challenging to work with in future interactions. Again, this is the kind of outlook that sabotages discussions before they begin. Whenever you go into a difficult conversation, recognize this bias and seek to listen as objectively as possible.

Be Profoundly Curious

When we are in conversation with people with whom we regularly disagree or simply do not like, we tend not to listen—and they know it. Why? Because we are convinced that we already know exactly what they are going to say. My advice is to leave the mind reading to the professionals. We have all heard a thousand times that active listening is important, but how do we do it in the face of all our biases, distractions, agendas, and tragically misinformed colleagues? The key to active listening is to become profoundly curious about what the other person has to say. This will completely alter your listening and the other person's experience of being heard. And there is a chance that your curiosity will pique theirs. The next time you find yourself thinking, *I already know what she is going to say*, consciously switch that thought to, *I have no idea what she is going to say, and I am incredibly curious to find out*. I remind myself whenever I speak to someone with whom I disagree, I am given the opportunity to learn something new, and, possibly, to change my views based on this information. I am not scared of people who change their views; I am scared of people who don't change their views when presented with new evidence to the contrary. Although I do not relish being proven wrong, I far prefer it to being closed-minded and ignorant. You will find that maintaining a curious mindset will have a profoundly positive impact when it comes to addressing disagreements in all aspects of your life.

Attack the Problem, Not the Person

During an argument, people can spend more time pointing fingers and attacking one another than focusing on the issues at hand. When people start blaming one another, it leads to an increase in emotions and subsequent decrease in calm and rational conversation. Imagine children fighting and a parent walking in and saying, "What is going on in here!" One child says, "He started it," and the other says, "She started it." Your boss does not care who started it; all he cares about is identifying and acting on the best solution possible, which will never happen in the midst of a blame-storming, finger-pointing match.

Get Off Your High Horse

Let's face it, there are times when we are in a discussion with someone, and we simply have greater knowledge of the subject. In fact, sometimes we try to expedite the conversation by saying, "Paul, you don't have my experience or expertise, so please listen to what I'm telling you." If you have ever been on the receiving end of such a comment or attitude, you know how offensive it is and how it only tends to fuel emotions. I do not know about you, but I have never responded, "John, you're absolutely right. I apologize for wasting your time by offering my uninformed thoughts. Please educate me." Obviously, if you truly have greater knowledge on the subject, use it as an opportunity to teach the other person. Just do not do so in a condescending manner. You might try saying, "Mimi, I've actually had quite a bit of experience dealing with these situations. I would like to share what I've learned and see if it might apply here." More critically, recognize and acknowledge when another person has more expertise on a subject than you do and be open to learning from her.

Exorcize the I-Am-in-Charge Mentality

The mindset of "I need to show them who is boss" is obviously a terrible one if you intend to foster collaboration. It is similar to the my-way-or-the-highway line of thinking. I once worked with a woman who was fond of saying, "There are two ways of doing things, my way or my way." Such posturing causes resentment and resistance, as well as a loss of respect for the individual. Particularly if you are in a leadership position, your mindset should always be that of a partner. Otherwise, you are likely going to be having a one-sided conversation. Your mindset should never be that you are better than anyone else. Stay humble.

Think Empathetically

When it comes to fostering positive relationships and dealing with conflict, there may be no more important mindset than that of empathy. Empathy allows us to understand what it feels like to be in others' shoes and to see things from their perspective, including their fears and concerns. Sometimes the person with whom we are having a conflict is in a tough and vulnerable position. For example, he made a mistake and is desperately trying to cover it up because he is afraid of being fired. If you demonstrate some empathy for whatever the person is dealing with, you can absolutely shift the conversation to one of collaboration.

Assume You Do Not Have All the Facts

Have you ever gotten into a heated discussion with someone and realized that either you or the other person did not have a complete understanding of the situation? Many conflicts arise because people assume that they have all the facts when they do not. My advice is to enter all critical conversations with the assumption that you do *not* have all the data because you likely do not. And you certainly do not know what you do not know. A great way to begin a conversation is to say, "I'd like to share what I know about the situation, so that you can tell me what I'm missing or may have gotten wrong." Now that is how you foster a healthy dialogue!

Assume You Do Not Have the Best Answer

A truly dangerous mindset is to believe that you have the best answer. I once asked a plant manager I was coaching for his biggest weakness. He responded that he thought he was always right and it kept him from listening to his employees' ideas and coming up with potentially better solutions. I think it is fair to say that lots of managers, leaders, and business owners believe they have the best answer, which, quite frankly, they might; however, they will not know if they do not elicit and consider others' ideas. Moreover, making unilateral decisions clearly sends the message to employees that their ideas are inferior and unwanted, which leads to their becoming demoralized and disengaged. Making decisions that affect people without asking for their input significantly diminishes their sense of ownership and commitment. When you do ask for team members' thoughts and suggestions, never give your own first, as doing so will reduce both the number and diversity of responses. Also, avoid the famous, "We've tried that before and it didn't work" line, as well as being overly critical of others' input as doing so will seriously inhibit future contributions. If your mind is already made up, then go with it. Asking people for their thoughts with no intention of using them is a waste of time, demoralizing, and disrespectful.

Consider That You Might Be Wrong

Consider, if only briefly, the possibility that you might be wrong. I am not suggesting that you walk around thinking this all the time; that would be fairly weird, and you might find yourself at a traffic light unsure of what to do. Rather, prior to and during a critical conversation, entertain the thought that your strongly held beliefs might actually be flawed. Trust me, this may be a hard one to swallow, but this mindset will free you from acting in all kinds of stubborn ways. Just imagine the impact of saying to yourself or, better yet, out loud, "You know what, I just might be wrong" during a heated exchange. It is not that you are giving up on your position; you are simply showing how open you are to considering additional facts and the other person's perspective. How might you respond if an antagonist said that to you?

Focus on What Is Possible

If you are the highlighting type, I suggest pulling out your marker. This mindset and approach has helped me in many personal and professional situations. How many times have you made a request and been told some version of, "No, that isn't possible"? I do not know about you, but I get really frustrated by such a response. It feels like the other person is trying to shut the door on me and the conversation. I find it quite rude. When confronted with this kind of verbal stop sign, I reply, "I got it. That option is not possible. Now, I would like to discuss what *is* possible." Such a reaction continues the conversation, and you would be amazed at how often a favorable resolution is reached. In fact, sometimes one that is even more desirable than your initial request.

Share Your View

As discussed in the chapter on cognitive biases, your view of the world is completely unique from anyone else's, and clearly, everyone else's is distinct from yours. In the context of constructive and collaborative conversations, it is critical to embrace the belief that your views and opinions are no more right than those of others. Similarly, your truth is not necessarily the truth for others. People draw entirely different conclusions based on exactly the same facts or evidence—just listen to any political debate. Thus, during conversations, especially those fueled by emotion, refrain from declaring that your view is the right view. Instead, say, "I would like to share my thoughts with you." Such a statement reflects humility and fosters collaboration.

Seek Progress

The underpinnings of interpersonal conflict typically build up over time through many less-than-ideal exchanges. As you work on a strained relationship with a colleague, do not set expectations too high; weeks, months, or even years of ill feelings are not going to magically disappear during a single conversation. At the same time, you should maintain a positive mindset geared toward making progress with each discussion. Similarly, when it comes to resolving complex issues, avoid thinking that you need to resolve all aspects in a single conversation. That is unrealistic and will likely lead to significant frustration. Instead, embrace a mindset that favors incremental progress. As I am fond of saying:

The difference between something and nothing is everything.

Give People a Break

Several years ago, I attended a workshop led by a Benedictine monk. At the end of the workshop, he pointed to each of us and said, "Here's what I know. Every person in this room is getting along in the world the best way he or she knows how." I remind myself of this message whenever I get frustrated or angry with someone. No one gets out of bed in the morning and declares, "I am so excited to go out into the world and make someone miserable today!" (If you know someone who does, stay as far away as possible.) Nearly all of us have significant stressors in our lives, such as those related to finances and the health and wellness of ourselves and our loved ones. Much of this book was written during the beginning months of the COVID-19 pandemic, and we all had a lot more on our minds than just work—unless, of course, we did not have any. If you are going to go into a critical conversation with any mindset, make it this:

> *Assume that the person you are sitting across from is a decent, hardworking, well-intentioned person getting along in the world the best way he or she knows how, just like you.*

By the way, you may want to give yourself a break as well.

SUMMARY

I may not know you personally, but I know something very important about you: namely, that you have a learning mindset, which may be the most important one of all. An openness to learning is critical when it comes to dealing with difficult people and conversations, but perhaps even more so in life. The tips in this chapter will help you promote healthy conversations and relationships with closed-minded individuals and will contribute to your ability to hold healthy conversations with your colleagues, no matter what their mindset.

UP NEXT

The following chapter will teach you the specific skills and strategies that will allow you to turn any difficult conversation into a healthy one. Time to get out your favorite highlighter again!

109

ON YOUR PLAYING FIELD

1. Think about times in which you found yourself heading into a difficult conversation. What are some negative mindsets that you brought with you? How do you think they impacted the course of the conversation?
2. Which mindsets discussed do you think would be the most challenging for you to adopt? Why is that? How might you overcome your resistance to doing so?
3. Imagine being in a heated discussion with someone. Which mindsets would be most important for you to embrace?
4. Ask to speak with someone at work who you know disagrees with you about a topic. Think of each mindset as a hat, and before going to the meeting, put on at least three of them. After the meeting is over, ask yourself whether you had a healthy and productive conversation and which of the "hats" were most helpful.

CHAPTER 10

COMMUNICATION SKILLS AND STRATEGIES

Interpersonal issues simply do not resolve on their own. As the saying goes, "Hope is not a strategy." The successful navigation of challenging conversations depends on one's ability to skillfully employ communication tactics and strategies. This chapter will provide you with the tools you need to have healthy and productive conversations. While I would expect that you are familiar with and may even use many of them unconsciously, you are sure to come across some new ones to add to your conversation toolbox. Even more importantly, many of these strategies can be used to prevent the need to have difficult conversations in the first place. As you read the chapter, consider how you may begin immediately implementing its content in your daily interactions.

Stick with the Facts

As discussed in the chapter on cognitive biases, it is remarkable how differently people can interpret the same facts. Stick with what you heard and saw as much as possible. Start difficult conversations by seeking a common understanding of and agreement on the key facts. For example, "I want to make sure that we are on the same page regarding the situation. From what I understand, Alex promised Kim that he would have his team finish maintenance on the conveyor during the night shift, but when she came in this morning it was still down. Is that your understanding?" Establishing clarity and facts from the get-go helps set the stage for a productive and collaborative conversation; otherwise, you are more likely to get stuck in a cycle of "he said, she said."

Stay Present and Take Note of the Impact on Others

Earlier in the book, we discussed how avoiding difficult conversations impacts other team members. Reminding people of this can be a very helpful strategy in encouraging them to resolve conflict. For example, "Tom, we obviously have our differences and we need to resolve them, preferably sooner rather than later. I am concerned that our disagreements are negatively impacting staff like Juanita, who is being given contradictory information and direction. My request is that you and I deal with issues directly and not involve our team members. Can you agree to that?" This technique contextualizes your conversation, which may help the other person become more aware of the bigger picture and more willing to reach a resolution.

Be Willing to Compromise

Some people have the mindset that they never compromise and may begin the conversation letting you know so. These people are like stubborn donkeys who dig their heels in and refuse to budge. Do you know anyone like that? If so, you understand how challenging they can be. Do not be one of them. If you are unwilling to compromise, then you are probably not very interested in seeking to understand others' perspectives or collaborating. If you think that standing your ground is a productive strategy, just consider how well it works with our elected officials in Washington, DC. Focus on the needs of your organization and customers before your own needs. Some people think that compromising leads to both parties losing; I have never seen it that way. Compromise often leads to better solutions that both can partially, if not fully, support. Making progress is almost always superior to standing still and staring at one another from across a table—or aisle. In the end, it is about the team winning and not the individual, and compromise allows that to happen.

Elephant? What Elephant?

The size and color of the elephant may be up for discussion, but his presence is usually undeniable. I am sure this will surprise you, but I recommend being quite straightforward when it comes to elephants, especially because they are usually not wearing camouflage and hiding in the lunchroom. For example, if I was in an ongoing conflict with a colleague, I might say, "I am going to state the obvious: we don't see eye to eye and haven't for a long time. People have shared that you have spoken negatively about me and my department, and unfortunately, I have spoken critically about you and your team. For that I apologize. The way I see it, our job is to do the best we can for this company and our employees, and I don't think we can do that if we are constantly setting up roadblocks for one another. I realize that I have been more concerned with making you wrong than I have been in acting professionally and in the best interest of the company. As of today, I am committing to treating you respectfully and to being the best business partner possible. And if I'm not acting in a manner consistent with that commitment, please tell me." If you sincerely want to reset a relationship with long-standing discord, you must address the matter head-on. Not that the past will be forgotten, but in less than 60 seconds, you can put the relationship on an entirely different trajectory. By the way, do not expect your response to be reciprocated. In fact, you may even get something like, "I'm glad that you've finally acknowledged what a jerk you are!" Breathe.

Stay on Point

Make sure to keep the conversation on track and focused on the present. Do not bring up the past unless it is clearly relevant to addressing the current situation. Since there is often a history of conflict between people, it is easy to digress and discuss other unresolved issues. To get the conversation back on track, try saying, "I agree, that is definitely something that we should deal with. However, it seems to take us away from what we agreed to focus on during this meeting. My request is that we discuss that topic at the end or schedule another time to give the matter the attention it deserves. Are you willing to do that?" Obviously, crystalizing the purpose of the meeting up front will help prevent it from drifting.

Be Concise

While staying on point, be as concise as possible. Most people are not very good at listening, and this is especially true when they are in an emotionally heightened state. Thus, you have even less of their attention than usual, so make good use of it by being as succinct as possible. Often, when we are emotional, we tend to ramble, which is a problem for a couple of reasons. First, key points get watered down and lost to the listener. Second, if you say something that the listener wants to comment on, build upon, or ask questions about, they will have a hard time paying attention to what you say after that point. Also, by the time they get the opportunity to speak, they may have forgotten what they wanted to say, or it may be irrelevant. (When interacting with a rambler, jot your thoughts down on a piece of paper so you do not have to worry about remembering them.) Third, rambling can come across to the listener as disrespectful because you seem interested only in hearing yourself speak and disinterested in the other's views. People who express themselves succinctly are perceived as being more knowledgeable, confident, and professional.

Highly extroverted individuals like me can have a hard time being succinct because we like to think out loud. Before important conversations or meetings, I always prepare by putting my main thoughts down on paper, and I practice presenting them as concisely and clearly as possible. Sometimes I will also acknowledge this propensity to my listener and ask that she interrupt me at will. For example, "I can get really caught up in what I'm saying and end up rambling and dominating a conversation, which I don't want to do. If you feel that I am, please just cut me off."

If you are speaking with a rambler, try breaking in by using one of the following statements:

- ► "Sorry for jumping in, but I think that is a really important point, and I wanted to piggyback on it."

- ► "Excuse me for interrupting, but I'd like to ask a question."

- ► "I apologize, but I want to make sure that I fully understand what you are suggesting."

After purposely interrupting in this way, it is easier to begin offering your thoughts without offending the other person.

Be Fiercely Clear

Ambiguity is the enemy of a productive conversation. Often, we think we are being clear when we are not. Making sure that others accurately understand what you are trying to communicate is critical, especially during tense conversations. But asking, "Do you understand?"

is a terrible way to do it as the question almost always elicits a "Yes," whether or not the other person actually understands. Also, depending on the context, asking someone if they understand can come across as a bit of a test to which answering "No" earns a failing grade. This is especially true if you are speaking to direct reports who may not want to admit ignorance for fear of looking bad. When it comes to assessing someone's understanding, you want to avoid asking questions that allow for a yes or no response. Say instead, "I have been told that I am not always as clear as I think I am. To make sure that we are on the same page, please tell me how you interpreted what I said." As a way of being proactive, whenever I begin working with a new client, I say up front that if I am ever being unclear or vague to please let me know.

Focus on Areas of Agreement

Typically, during emotional conversations, people focus immediately on differences of opinion. Instead, begin by focusing on any areas of agreement, no matter how small or minor. For example, "Can we agree that the priority should be on satisfying the customer?" As much as possible, demonstrate that you are aligned in achieving the same outcome. You might even point to similar beliefs within an area of disagreement. (Sounds odd, I know.) For example, "While we may differ in terms of our strategies to expand the businesses, the most important point is that we both agree we need to do so." The more areas of agreement you identify, the more likely you are to collaborate rather than argue. Just do not agree to disagree!

Consistently Self-Monitor

Throughout the conversation, check in with yourself and evaluate your behavior as a communication partner. Keep in mind the acronym WAIT: Why Am I Talking? Ask yourself the following "Am I" questions as you self-assess:

► Am I really adding value to the conversation?

► Am I giving the other person the time he needs and deserves to share his views?

► Am I really listening to the other person, or am I just listening to the voice inside my head?

► Am I really open to considering different opinions?

► Am I letting my natural biases cloud my judgment?

► Am I just being stubborn?

► Am I judging the other person unfairly?

► Am I asking relevant and meaningful questions to understand the other person's perspective?

► Am I paraphrasing to demonstrate active listening and ensure understanding?

► Am I practicing body language that conveys active interest and respect?

► Am I truly committed to a healthy conversation?

In general, put yourself in the other person's shoes, and imagine what it is like to communicate with you. Would you feel heard?

Say What You Have to Say, and Do Not Say What You Do Not Need to Say

Preparing for difficult conversations is important. It not only helps you identify what you plan to say, it helps clarify what you will *not* say. In general, but especially during a tense conversation, if you think, "I wonder if I should say that?" the answer is probably "No." There is often more potential downside than upside when you have not fully thought through your response. You can always share your comments and opinions later, but you cannot take back words you have spoken. Trust me, I have tried. "I didn't mean it that way" rarely gets me off the hook. Knowing when not to speak is a critical communication skill and can make or break a conversation.

Be Candid

Always be straightforward, but never be a jerk. When we feel that the other person is withholding information or beating around the bush, we get suspicious, our level of trust decreases, and we wonder what he is really thinking and what else he may not be saying. For example, imagine giving an important presentation, after which you ask a colleague for her thoughts, and she responds, "I thought it was fine." I do not know about you, but that is not the answer I was hoping for. "Fine" is what people say to be nice. If I were asked this question by a close colleague and had constructive feedback to offer, I would say something like, "John, I'll be honest. You seemed a bit nervous and didn't come across as confidently as I have seen you in the past. Unfortunately, I'm not sure that you got your key points across as clearly and strongly as you probably wanted to." While it may make me cringe, I always appreciate when people give me candid feedback because I know that it will make me better.

Float Your Ideas

This tip is helpful to test the waters, and potentially avoid a difficult conversation down the road. Imagine, for example, that you plan on making a change to a process that will likely impact the work of a colleague or direct report. Obviously, the worst thing you can do is make the decision with no input. *Always talk about it.* If you are going to discuss what may be a hot-topic issue for the other person, approach it carefully. You might say, for example, "I'd like to run something by you," or "I've been thinking about something and would really like to

COMMUNICATION SKILLS AND STRATEGIES

get your input." Such statements invite conversation and decrease the likelihood of a defensive or contentious response. However, if the decision has already been made, then do not act as though it has not, or, you may have just created what will really be a difficult conversation!

Ask Questions

It is critical during fraught conversations to demonstrate that you are engaged and authentically interested in what the other person has to say. There is no simpler way to do this than by asking questions. The more targeted the question, the more it demonstrates that you are listening. Avoid the statement, "I don't know what you're talking about." It is totally unhelpful. Here's an example of a targeted question aimed at receiving more clarity: "You mentioned that the vendor had never done *this* before. Can you be more specific?" Obviously, the more questions you ask, the more you will learn about a given situation and the other person's perspective, which promotes collaboration and informs problem solving. There is rarely any downside to sincerely asking questions. Unfortunately, sometimes we choose not to ask them because we feel that doing so may make us appear uninformed. When I worry about looking bad, I say, "I realize this may reveal my ignorance, but can you help me understand . . ." By the way, asking such a question also has the added benefit of creating a sense of vulnerability which tends to decrease conflict.

Paraphrase, Paraphrase, Paraphrase

There may be no more effective technique in all of communication than paraphrasing. Similar to asking questions, paraphrasing lets the other person know that you are both listening and comprehending. It shows respect and increases the likelihood that the other person will actively listen to you. Simply use the following sentence structure: "Let me make sure I understand what you are saying . . ." The statement should be made in a calm, objective, and concise manner. Also, make sure to establish direct eye contact while speaking, as this demonstrates you are fully present and engaged in the conversation. A word of caution: be careful that when you paraphrase you do not come across as interrupting and rushing the speaker. If your intention *is* to cause a break in the conversation, then paraphrasing works well. If, however, you simply want to demonstrate that you are paying attention and comprehending what the other person is saying, wait until she has finished speaking before you begin.

Let Yourself Be Vulnerable

Sometimes you can use vulnerability as a communication strategy to decrease tension in a conversation or to prevent it from occurring in the first place. Psychologically, when you open yourself up, you decrease the other person's aggression. A classic example from the animal kingdom is a dog rolling on its back and exposing its belly, making it extremely vulnerable. (To be clear, I am not recommending doing this at work!) This strategy can be highly effective during tense conversations or to prevent them from occurring in the first place. For example, imagine dealing with a situation that you worry may rub a colleague the wrong way. You might say something like: "I have to be honest. I am embarrassed to even ask you this, but I think I'm in over my head and could really use your help." It is far more difficult for another person to become angry when presented with such a hat-in-hand posture.

Do Not Be Afraid to Say, "I Don't Know"

During heated discussions, people may ask questions to test or embarrass the other person. They may also ask questions to which there is no good, or even possible, answer. Such questions can be meant to intimidate or confuse the listener. Imagine someone saying in a loud voice: "Really? Really? Is that what you think?!" or "Since you seem to know everything around here, you tell me how those spare parts magically disappeared!" Under such circumstances, "I don't know" is a perfectly good answer. If you are going to insert a "but," be careful. If you are asked, "Do you seriously have any idea how we got to those numbers?" A good response is, "I don't, but I would appreciate it if you helped me understand that." A poor response is, "I don't, but I'm guessing you do." There are also rhetorical questions to which no response is expected. For example, "Do you have any idea how incredibly stupid that answer was and how bad it made our company look?" The bottom line is, if you do not know the answer to a question, be straight and say so. I always respect people when they admit without embarrassment their lack of knowledge. How about you?

Let Them Vent

While I strongly suggest that you vent alone, with a pet, or to a friend, there are times when allowing others to vent may be just what they need. When people are incredibly angry, they simply are not in a mindset to have any kind of conversation, and they are certainly not interested in your thoughts or needs. Give others the time they need to express their frustrations and wear themselves out. If you are familiar with the boxing strategy of "rope-a-dope" made famous by Muhammad Ali, then you know what I am talking about. (If you are not familiar, it means to let the other person punch themselves to exhaustion, or in this case, rant until they are all ranted out.) While someone is venting, just listen and remain absolutely calm. When he is finished, you may want to make an empathetic statement and then begin to systematically address his concerns. For example, "You're right. Having to wait six weeks to be reimbursed for your expenses is not right, and I would be upset as well. I am going to take care of this as soon as we get off the phone and will follow up as soon as I know when payment will be made. Is there anything else I can do?" Whatever you do, do not say, "Are you done yet?" Obviously, if the individual venting becomes aggressive and overly contentious, then remove yourself from the situation. Otherwise, recognize that venting is, many times, a necessary precursor to a less emotional and more levelheaded conversation.

Validate Feelings

During almost all emotionally charged conversations, the other person does not feel understood. Never tell someone that they do not have a right to feel a certain way. Stay away from phrases like, "I don't know why you're upset," or "Just calm down. You are making a big deal out of nothing." When people feel validated, understood, and respected, they will be less defensive and more collaborative. If you are an authentically empathetic person, use the following simple phrase to validate another's emotions: "I would feel the same way in your shoes." Such an empathetic statement is particularly appropriate when people feel as though agreements were made and broken—for example, they were promised the opportunity to participate in the company's high-potential program, but when the list came out, they were not on it. Obviously, do what you can to address, fix, or otherwise help the other person understand the "why" behind the broken promise. If the person is extremely upset and screaming, do not say anything. Your attempt to validate her feelings might lead to a retort such as, "Really? Really! Well, if that were the case, you wouldn't have let it happen in the first place!" If you are not a particularly empathetic person, you may be best off sincerely saying, "I am sorry that you feel that way."

"I Am Confused and Concerned"

In *Carrots and Sticks Don't Work*, I introduced the phrase, "I'm confused and concerned," and it has become one of the most highlighted sections of the book on the Kindle edition. This approach can be used with direct reports, colleagues, vendors, customers, and even your boss. Here I will give a detailed example of working with a direct report, but feel free to adjust the dialogue based on the relationship.

Imagine a manager who has assigned a task to a direct report and it has not been completed. In most cases, the manager approaches the employee with an accusatory, "Why didn't you get this done?" Depending on the tone, this can come across as highly critical and immediately lead the direct report to become defensive. Such a question often comes across as attacking the person and not the problem. If you believe that the employee is incompetent, being passive-aggressive, or purposely screwing up, then you should put him on a personal improvement plan or fire him. If, however, you believe that the employee is a hardworking individual who wants to do a good job, then I suggest a different approach. First and foremost, assume that you are not as good a communicator as you think and were unclear with at least some aspect of your request. The number one reason that an individual fails to complete a task is because she did not fully understand it in the first place. Second, assume, that you do not have all the facts. Third, remind yourself that your job is to get the best out of your team members, and their failures are your failures. Making them feel incompetent or beating them up is not part of your job description.

Assuming that you want to be a supportive manager and help your people succeed, use the framework of "I am confused and concerned." For example, "I am confused because I thought I was clear when I asked you to get the presentation done by today, and I am concerned because that doesn't seem to be what happened. Am I missing something? Can you help me understand where you are with this?" If it turns out that the employee was not clear regarding the task, did not have the resources or information available to complete it, or was confronted with an emergency, then you should take these facts into consideration and reset expectations. Obviously, the employee should have kept you informed of such issues and her inability to meet the deadline. As discussed, make sure the employee knows the reason behind the request and, if applicable, why you are asking it to be completed in a particular manner. If her performance does not improve after the "confused and concerned" conversation, then another one laying out the appropriate consequences should follow.

Take a Time-Out

I realize this is not the first time that we have talked about a time-out, and it will not be the last. It is simply one of the most effective techniques when dealing with an emotionally charged situation and individual. There are three primary reasons to call a time-out. First, to prepare for the conversation, especially when someone attempts to engage you in a spontaneous discussion. Second, to allow time for your own emotions or those of the other to abate. Third, when you feel that you are at an impasse and no further progress will be made during the conversation. It is important that both parties feel comfortable calling a time-out at any time. Even if this is not a specifically articulated ground rule, you should always feel empowered to request a break, and you should always honor another's request to do so. As discussed, when you feel the need to step away, use language such as, "I would appreciate taking some time to gather my thoughts." If you sense that the other person's emotions are rising, suggest a time-out by saying, "It seems as though it might be helpful for us both to collect our thoughts a bit more and continue this conversation tomorrow." I look back at times in my life when I should have called a time-out and regretted not having done so. As you get deeper into an emotional conversation, especially when you feel intimidated, you can begin to feel paralyzed. My suggestion is to gain separation as soon as you feel triggered; do not wait too long or it may be too late.

Once secured, use your time-out productively. As a starting point, catch your breath, relax, and put things into perspective. If you need to vent, fine, but keep it short because it is unlikely to be productive. Consider engaging friends and/or close colleagues to discuss the situation. Be prepared that a reality check might reveal that you are more culpable than you thought. In fact, you may end up apologizing to the other person. Consider it a blessing to have friends willing to give you such honest feedback.

Another good way to spend your breather is collecting additional facts—and not just ones that support your view so that you can prove the other person wrong! During the time-out, consider reviewing the tips from prior chapters and make sure that you have a productive mindset and are conscious of your biases and push buttons. Once you reengage in the conversation, make sure to begin on a collaborative note, and, if authentic, apologize for your behavior during the initial discussion. For example, "Pete, thanks for agreeing to continue our conversation now. I realize that I was being stubborn and focused more on trying to get you to agree with me than being interested in what you had to say. I apologize." In the span of about 11 seconds (I timed myself), you have completely changed the tenor of the conversation and dramatically increased the likelihood of it being a productive one.

SUMMARY

Healthy conversations don't just happen. Being in a critical conversation in which both you and the other person feel strongly and passionately about an issue and turning it into a calm and collaborative discussion takes skill. This chapter, as well as elements of prior chapters, has provided you with the tools that will improve your skill and make you more effective. Please note: the vast majority of the tactics and strategies outlined in this chapter are intended to be used in everyday conversations—not just ones that you view as difficult.

UP NEXT

At this point in the book, I hope that you are feeling a bit more willing and confident in your ability to address what you may perceive to be a difficult conversation. In the Introduction, I asked you to think about situations that you may be avoiding, I promised by the end of this book that you would be able to navigate them. The next chapter will guide you through preparing for the conversation to concluding it; as the expressions goes, from soup to nuts.

ON YOUR PLAYING FIELD

1. Look back through the many tactics in this chapter and identify those that you feel would be of greatest use to you.
2. Over the next week, focus on using these tactics in both your personal and professional conversations. I challenge you to practice each chosen tactic five times.
3. When using these skills, do you feel more empowered and in charge of yourself and the conversation? And if so, why do you think that is?

CONVERSATION ROAD MAP

Conversations are journeys with lots of opportunities to get sidetracked and lost. In the immortal words of Yogi Berra, "If you don't know where you are going, you might wind up someplace else." And, when it comes to relationships and critical conversations, you may easily end up at an undesirable destination. So, just as with planning a trip, map out your route from the beginning to the end. While you cannot perfectly script a conversation, particularly one that is likely to evoke some emotion, this chapter provides a general framework for keeping your discussions on track and maximally productive. (See Appendix B for several scripted conversations.)

Decide Whether to Engage or Disengage

While most of the time we rationalize avoiding difficult conversations, there are instances in which it would be more prudent to refrain from addressing an issue. Take the following steps to decide whether to engage in a discussion or let it go.

Chill

As previously discussed, when you get emotionally triggered, your sympathetic nervous system kicks in and your body literally heats up. When you start feeling hotheaded, take time to cool off. Until you quiet your emotions and your mind, you will be unable to thoughtfully assess the situation, identify your options, and decide on the best course of action.

Assess the Situation

Once you have calmed down and can think more objectively, process the situation. Take the time to analyze what was said and/or done, the context, and where things stand. Then ask yourself the following questions:

Is this issue really worth getting upset about? After you step away and take a breath, you may realize that the issue is simply not a big deal and addressing it would make it a bigger one. For example, you perceived a colleague's comment as unnecessarily critical during a meeting, but once you gave it some thought, you recognized that you were probably just being overly sensitive.

Am I the problem? Take a look in the mirror and ask yourself whether you might be the source of the conflict. Did your words or actions trigger your colleague? Maybe you said something that elicited that snide comment. Perhaps it is you who owes the other person an apology. It is important to be self-aware enough to recognize and take responsibility for your own role in spurring conflict.

Is the behavior out of character? It may be that the other person is struggling with a challenging situation and is taking his frustrations out on you. Instead of being upset, perhaps some empathy would be the best response. For example: "Harry, it seems that you haven't been yourself lately. I don't want to pry, but if there is anything that you would like to talk about or I can help you with, please let me know." A little empathy can go a long way in fostering healthy relationships and recognizing when others are hurting, rather than actively trying to hurt you.

What is the potential upside versus downside of addressing the issue? How much do you have to lose versus gain? What benefits might the conversation produce, assuming it goes well? Is there a genuine risk that addressing the situation will worsen the relationship? Make sure to avoid unlikely and overly pessimistic thinking. You may want to run your thoughts by a friend or team member and get his or her input.

Is there good reason to believe that your conversation may lead to negative consequences for another? Imagine a friend at work shares that another team member is spreading lies about you. Naturally, you would be upset and want to confront that individual. However, doing so may put your friend at risk for possible retribution. When others are involved, as they often are, remember to consider how your decisions may impact them.

Are there other legitimate considerations? For example, are there office politics that would make addressing an issue or individual imprudent? Or impending organizational changes that would favor a wait-and-see approach?

Make a Decision

Once you have reflected on each of these questions, write down a list of all the pros and cons of addressing versus not addressing the issue. If you choose not to pursue a conversation, then you need to let go of the matter. You cannot play martyr or lay claim to being the bigger person. You are not allowed to be resentful toward yourself or your colleague. Also, recognize that just because you decide against initiating a discussion does not mean the other person will make the same decision. If a team member asks to speak about the issue, honor her request.

Preparation

The outcome of a difficult conversation often depends on the quality of your preparation. Doing anything on the fly leaves the outcome more susceptible to emotional outbursts and uncertainty. Just as you would not participate in a sporting event or theater production without preparation, you should never begin a critical conversation without first developing a well-thought-out game plan. In the words often attributed to Benjamin Franklin, "By failing to prepare, you are preparing to fail." While preparation does not guarantee a perfect outcome, it will certainly increase the likelihood of a productive conversation.

Determine Your Goals

What do you want to accomplish as a result of the conversation? What is your main objective or goal(s)? I find that many people spend too little time thinking about this question and end up in venting sessions rather than productive discussions. Is your desired outcome for the other person to fully understand and consider your perspective? Is it for you to understand and appreciate the other's point of view? Is your goal to turn an argument into a brainstorming session or to reach a compromise? Maybe your intention is simply to apologize. Under no circumstances should your end goal be to secure another person's apology or admission of fault.

Begin with a Healthy Mindset

As you prepare for the conversation, make sure you enter it with a healthy mindset, taking into consideration all the tips in Chapter 9. Unfortunately, as you know, our default is to maintain our unconscious biases and negative attitudes toward the other person. It is easier to point a finger than look in the mirror. Review and embrace the elements of a healthy conversation. Remember, our beliefs going into a situation greatly influence the experience and outcome, so be very intentional in thinking that the discussion will be a respectful, collaborative, and constructive one.

Request a Meeting

I suggest requesting a meeting by email rather than in person or over the phone. Always make sure to let the other person know why you are asking to speak. For example: "I would appreciate 30 minutes to discuss the accident report you filed yesterday. Do you have a window of time in the late afternoon? If not, when would be most convenient for you?" In general, you want to arrange for a conversation as soon as possible after the triggering event. If you think the person may become upset as a result of the conversation, consider scheduling the discussion at the end of the day so she has time to process what has been said and is not distracted in subsequent meetings. Allow more time than you think will be necessary, so you never have to worry about cutting a critical conversation short. If in person, meet in a private space, away from prying eyes. If you are conducting a videoconference, ensure privacy and discretion by preventing background distractions, such as others walking into view. If your organization uses public calendars, you may want to block off time to speak about a delicate issue by simply marking that time period with a generic "busy." While I find that nearly all critical conversations are held between two people, there may be times when having others present makes sense, especially if they are directly involved with and impacted by the issue at hand.

Communicate the Agenda

Once a meeting time has been agreed upon, send an invite. The subject line should reflect the reason for the meeting, such as, "Discuss yesterday's incident report." Keep it simple, clear, and devoid of any words that might evoke emotion. Begin the email by addressing the recipient by name. Include a brief agenda, perhaps just a few key bullet points; do not send a long, detailed agenda with time frames. Your goal is to lay the foundation for a conversation, not a formal meeting. Make sure to express the following sentiment, "Please let me know if we are on the same page and if there is anything else you would like to add." When closing the email, do *not* say, "I look forward to speaking" because, in reality, you probably do not and neither does the other person. Rather, simply sign off with a more genuine, "Regards, Paul."

Write Down Your Key Points

Prepare written or typed notes that include your key points. Doing so allows you to be clear and succinct and diminishes the likelihood of you rambling and straying from the agenda.

Practice the Conversation

Visualization and role-playing should be standard elements of your preparation. Just as you would learn a role in a play or train in advance of a sporting match, practicing how you intend the conversation to go will dramatically increase the likelihood of it going that way. Ideally, role-play with someone familiar with both the situation and the other person, so that she can respond as realistically as possible. Make sure to build in scenarios in which the discussion goes astray and work out how best to get it back on track. The more important the conversation, the more time you should spend rehearsing, even if only by yourself. There is simply no substitute for practice.

During the Conversation

Once on the playing field, continue to focus on the main issues and objective(s) of the conversation and control what you can control: your actions and reactions. Maintain your positive mindset and remain calm and respectful at all times. While you will make many in-the-moment decisions, the following tactics will help you keep the conversation on track and productive.

Arrive Early

You never want to have to worry about rushing to a critical conversation. Whenever possible, avoid participating in a meeting that ends directly beforehand. If in the office, arriving early will allow you to choose where you want to sit and to get settled. You could also arrive early but allow the other person to choose her seat. Try to sit six to eight feet apart but not across from one another; being catty-corner on a rectangular table works best. Move your seat if necessary. Make sure that your phone is off and out of sight. Just as with an in-person meeting, do not be late to a video call. If, for any reason, you will be even a minute late, notify the other person via text or email as soon as possible.

Begin the Conversation Authentically

Do not start the conversation by saying, "How are you?" In fact, unless speaking to someone close to me, I never ask such a question because it almost always comes across as inauthentic. Culturally, we feel obliged to give a positive response, such as "I'm well," regardless of how the individual is really doing. Shortly after a loved one passed, I had a call with a client who casually and innocently asked how I was doing. While holding back tears, I said, "Oh, I'm fine. How are you?" In terms of opening pleasantries, I recommend saying, "I appreciate you making the time to speak with me," or "Good morning."

Frame the Conversation with Your Commitment to the Relationship

I cannot emphasize enough how essential this step is in setting the stage for a healthy and constructive conversation. Imagine the typical feelings and thoughts you have before entering what you believe will be an emotionally charged conversation. Imagine the other person having the same feelings and thoughts. Each person feels compelled to "win" by proving themselves right and the other wrong. (Visually,

I think of two rams clashing horns.) What if you took a totally differ-ent approach? What if you began the conversation by talking about the importance of the relationship rather than who was wrong or right? I have found any version of the following sentence extremely effective in reducing both aggressiveness and defensiveness: "I want you to know that I am fully committed to having a respectful and collaborative working relationship, starting with today's conversation." Imagine if someone said this to you. How would you respond? Obviously, the statement must be meant genuinely and sincerely. In fact, if you do not feel that way, do not say it. Incidentally, I have never had the other per-son say, "Well, I'm not really into working together. Let's just argue."

Keep to the Agenda

Before proceeding with the conversation, review the agreed-upon agenda and goals for the meeting—for example, "Cory, I just want to take a moment and make sure we are still on the same page regard-ing the focus of our discussion today." If there is disagreement on the agenda, ask questions to fully understand the other person's perspec-tive. Seek to shape the conversation so that both parties' needs are addressed. Then, adhere to the agenda as much as possible to avoid digressing into tangential issues. Sticking to the agenda will lead to a more efficient and productive conversation.

Come with and Take Notes During the Meeting

Have your prepared notes handy. Depending on the situation, you may want to take additional notes during the meeting to reference later. In person, use a paper notepad rather than a laptop or iPad because technology decreases interpersonal connectedness. During a video conversation, let the other person know that you will be glancing at or taking notes so they do not think you are distracted. Depending on your typing skills, you may be able to do this without looking down at the keyboard. (Obviously, your spelling and punctuation do not have to be perfect.) Eye contact is even more important during virtual meetings because your opportunity and ability to read nonverbal cues will be very limited, so take notes if appropriate, but maintain as much eye contact as possible. If you have dual monitors, keep your notes on one screen during the meeting and your video conference on the other. Toward the end of the meeting, review your list to ensure you have addressed each point. (Of course, during the course of the conversation, some points may have become irrelevant or better left unsaid.) In general, you will want to read through what you have written at the end of the conversation to ensure that you have accurately captured the key points. Doing so will reinforce to the other person that you were focused on the conversation during its duration and are serious about making positive change.

Make Sure That You Are Addressing the Big Issue

Sometimes we can focus too much on specific instances and either miss or ignore the big overarching issue that needs most to be addressed. As the expression goes, sometimes we cannot see the forest for the trees. I once had an extremely talented team member, Tomas, who would agree to a plan and later decide that he knew better and complete tasks his own way. I am all about initiative, but not when it contradicts what was agreed upon. As you might imagine, I am extremely open to discussing and revisiting decisions. Half the time, I would bite my tongue because Tomas was extremely hardworking and loyal, and replacing him would have been very difficult. And, quite frankly, he was more often right than wrong. Over time, however, I became increasingly frustrated by his behavior and my own inaction. One day, when he yet again diverged from the plan, it was the proverbial straw that broke the camel's back. I yelled in frustration and nearly fired him on the spot. After walking away, I had a bit of an epiphany. While I was certainly upset that Tomas did not come to me to discuss his intentions, there was a much bigger problem: I no longer trusted him. I could not trust him to keep his word, and that was the real problem that I needed to confront. When you avoid dealing with the big issues, you never solve the small ones.

Get at the Underlying or Root Cause of the Conflict

If your partner yells and screams when you spill the milk, it probably is not about the milk. Oftentimes, we deal with surface issues without addressing the underlying problem, which may or may not be known to us. For example, imagine a colleague with whom you were close beginning to distance herself from you. Or a team member with whom you always got along well suddenly becoming very disagreeable and antagonistic. When you see these kinds of changes in behavior, consider that there may be some underlying upset that needs to be addressed. In my experience, I find that it usually stems from the other person feeling disrespected. In such circumstances, you should seek to understand why the person is upset and initiate a conversation. You might say, for example, "Lev, I'm concerned because it seems that our relationship has recently become somewhat strained, and I am wondering if I did or said something that may have upset you. If so, I would very much appreciate you letting me know so that we can talk about it." Changes in how people relate to one another are almost always precipitated by some incident; if left unaddressed, the relationship will likely not improve.

Wrapping Up the Conversation

The conclusion of the conversation is just as important as how it started, if not more so. This is the moment to ensure that both parties agree on any key takeaways, decisions, commitments, and next steps. Gains made during the meeting will be lost if agreed-upon actions are not adhered to. The following suggestions will help you to conclude the conversation effectively and to shift successfully into the follow-up phase.

Review the Areas of Agreement

At the end of the conversation, make sure to review all the decisions and commitments that have been agreed upon by both parties. For example, "Phoebe, I want to make sure that we are in agreement. After this conversation, I am going to speak with Frank in operations and confirm that the order will be completed by Friday. I will then call shipping and confirm the departure and arrival date to the customer. I will get back to you by two o'clock. You will then reach out to the customer and give him the update. Did I get that right?" If, based on an equivocal response, you sense disagreement, continue the conversation until you are certain that there is full agreement on the plan.

Make a Request

At the end of almost every critical conversation, I make a specific request in hopes of preventing the same problem from recurring. For example, I might say, "I'm glad we had this conversation today and were able to resolve our differences. I want to request that in the future, if you disagree with a decision I have made, you come to me directly rather than to our boss. Are you willing to agree to that?" While a yes does not guarantee fidelity to the promise, it certainly demonstrates your desire for an open, straightforward, and mutually respectful relationship.

Set a Specific Follow-Up Time

Schedule the date and time for next steps or a check-in conversation. For example, "Carol, I think it would be helpful for us to schedule a follow-up conversation to ensure that we are staying on track. I definitely want to avoid finding ourselves in a similar situation. Does that make sense to you?" If you do not take this step, the next time you speak about the issue will likely be when there is another problem.

Express Your Gratitude for the Other Person's Willingness to Have the Conversation

Express your genuine appreciation for the other person's willingness to engage in the conversation, especially if he initiated it. I was once coaching a client, George, who angrily called me on the Monday after a Friday session to tell me how upset he was with something I had said. As you might imagine, I was extremely taken aback. I immediately felt myself becoming defensive, but I quickly let that go and focused on actively listening and understanding his concerns. After he stopped speaking, I said, "George, I am truly sorry that you were offended by what I said. I was trying to give you constructive feedback, but I can see how it came across as highly critical. I sincerely apologize." Once the conversation wound down and we reached an understanding, I made sure to express my gratitude: "George, I really want to thank you for letting me know that what I said upset you." If he had not had the courage to do so, I would not have had the opportunity to apologize and our relationship would likely never have been the same.

Follow Up in Writing

Have you ever had a conversation in which you and the other person had very different recollections of the details? I know I have. To help prevent that, send a follow-up email summarizing what was agreed upon and, of course, thank the other person for having had the conversation. At the same time, remember to send an invite for the ensuing meeting (if necessary).

Move On

Sometimes, despite your skill and competence for having a healthy conversation, the discussion is just not productive. Like having your car stuck deeply in the mud, there is no point in continuing to spin your wheels. At such times, I find it best to end the conversation by being direct: "Unfortunately, it doesn't feel as though we are any closer to an agreement now than we were a half-hour ago. I would like to suggest that we schedule another call for Friday afternoon. Between now and then, let's both spend time reflecting on what was discussed and see if there are any areas on which we might agree or compromise. Is that OK with you?" If you ever feel a conversation is not getting anywhere, it is better to take a break than risk it getting worse.

SUMMARY

Does all this sound like a lot for you to remember and act upon? It is. Did you ever consider how much really goes into having a healthy conversation? Dealing with conflict situations takes thought and work, if you want them to go well. As you prepare for any critical conversation, reread this and the previous chapter and take notes. As you engage in real-world conversations and put the content of these pages into action, you will become more and more competent and confident.

UP NEXT

All conversations occur within the context of a relationship. The healthier the relationship, the more likely you will have a healthy conversation. The following chapter will teach you how to build and maintain healthy relationships, and, if need be, restore them.

ON YOUR PLAYING FIELD

1. Think about an impending critical conversation and use this chapter to create an outline in preparation for the meeting. Make sure to be clear about your goals and what you want to achieve as a result of the discussion.

2. Share your outline with a trusted colleague and ask for constructive feedback. Make adjustments to your plan accordingly.

3. Use visualization and role-playing to practice different versions of the conversation. The more you practice, the more confident you will feel.

4. After having the actual conversation, debrief in detail with the colleague who helped you prepare. Review what went well and what did not. Discuss any surprises that may have come up and how you might have better prepared. Ask for suggestions on how best to handle situations with this person going forward.

CHAPTER 12

BUILDING, RESTORING, AND MAINTAINING HEALTHY RELATIONSHIPS

Whether it is your car, teeth, or relationships, maintenance is vital. Unfortunately, most people are better at getting their oil changed and teeth cleaned than they are at actively keeping relationships healthy and well-functioning. In fact, we often do not pay attention to how our relationships are working until they no longer do. Maintaining a healthy relationship greatly reduces conflict and confrontation because disagreements are handled in a timely, direct, and collaborative manner. While most of us would undoubtedly agree with the maxim that relationships take work, we do not always know the best way to work on them. How healthy are your relationships? What have you done recently to maintain them? In this chapter, we will discuss specific strategies to build, restore, and maintain healthy relationships.

Building New Relationships

It is far easier to build a healthy relationship from scratch than to rebuild a poor one. Taking the time needed at the outset to establish a strong foundation will pay dividends in the form of open communication, teamwork, and reduced risk of confrontation. The following will help you create connectedness and relatedness from the start, two staples of healthy relationships.

Step 1: Start on the Right Foot

When we begin new relationships, we often let them develop organically over time via experiences. My suggestion is to be more proactive and use your interpersonal skills to actively place the relationship on a healthy course right from the start. Consider the following analogy: we practice good oral hygiene because it increases our chances of having healthy gums and decreases the risk of disease. Why would we not do the same with our relationships?

A good place to begin is by mentally setting a very clear intention. For example, "My intention is to build a personal and highly collaborative working relationship with my new team member." Next, plan a strategy to meet your intention. Here is an example of how I might begin a conversation with a new colleague: "David, thanks for taking the time to chat with me. I remember my first two weeks and how hectic things were. Hopefully, you are beginning to settle in. I wanted to take some time to get more acquainted and see if I could help you out in any way."

Step 2: Establish Rapport

If you want to build a relationship, you must establish rapport, which occurs when there is a sense of connectedness and relatedness. The more we have in common with others, the more likely we will develop rapport with them. Even simply saying that you remember what your first two weeks were like is a way of signaling empathy around a shared experience. People can connect around all kinds of topics, including interests, hobbies, backgrounds, children, pets, or even a favorite vacation spot, musical group, or television show. The more personal the connection, the more quickly bonds are created. For example, when two people discover that they attended the same small college or overcame similar life challenges, rapport occurs promptly and naturally. So, when it comes to building or improving relationships, seek to identify those common life experiences that will have you feeling genuinely connected to the other person. The following are some statements and questions that you might ask over time:

- ► How did you find out about the open position?

- ► What made you decide to take the job?

- ► Tell me about your background, e.g., personal, educational, professional.

- ► Tell me about your family. (You should seek to learn about the significant people in your new colleague's life, e.g., the names of her partner, children, and pets. If the person has children, you may want to ask their ages or what grades they are in school.)

- ► What do you like to do outside of work?

Most people are comfortable sharing this information, but do not push if the person seems hesitant or uncomfortable. Always respect boundaries. Do not make your first conversation sound like an interrogation, and reciprocate by sharing about yourself. As you build trust and familiarity, continue to ask questions and engage in conversations that help you learn more about one another and what you each find important.

Step 3: Create a Foundation of Trust

Healthy relationships cannot exist without a strong foundation of trust. The lack of such a foundation is the number one reason that relationships break down. A good place to start is by establishing your own integrity and reliability. Ask yourself these questions:

- ► Can people trust me to keep my word, no matter what and no matter how small the matter?

- ► Am I reliable?

  - ▷ If you tell someone that you will meet her at 10:00 a.m., do you show up by 10:00 a.m., or do you saunter in or appear on screen with a fresh cup of coffee at 10:05 a.m.?

  - ▷ Do you tell people that you will get back to them by the end of the day, but then things always seem to prevent you from keeping that commitment?

  - ▷ Have you ever said that you would follow up on an issue and forgot? Worse yet, said you did when you had not?

Additionally, ask yourself if people can trust you to be competent and have the skills necessary to deliver on your promises. There are times when, quite frankly, people are put in positions where they simply do not have the education and experience to succeed. If you find yourself being asked to complete a task for which you are not qualified, be honest about it or you will definitely lose both trust and respect. While it is extremely important for colleagues to trust your word, it is equally important for you to trust theirs. Healthy relationships must have shared trust; they simply cannot exist without it.

Restoring Relationships

Unfortunately, relationships can erode over time, get off track, or otherwise become unhealthy, tense, and stressful. In such cases, action needs to be taken to restore them to a healthy state of mutual trust and respect. While not all relationships are salvageable, the following steps will help put you on a better path.

Step 1: Assess the Health of the Relationship

The first step in restoring or maintaining a healthy relationship is assessing its current state. While I am not a fan of the traditional performance review, I am an advocate of relationship reviews. Healthy relationships are characterized by mutual trust, respect, and support; honest and direct conversations; and a willingness to compromise. Such relationships produce healthy conversations, so disagreements are less likely to turn into arguments and issues are resolved quickly without drama. In a healthy relationship, difficult conversations become a lot less difficult and a lot less frequent.

Imagine that you and a colleague have very different ideas about how to deal with an irate customer. In an unhealthy relationship, this would lead to conflict rather than brainstorming because each person would have little interest in understanding and exploring the merits of the other's viewpoint. In contrast, when disagreements occur between people in a healthy relationship, there is open and straightforward dialogue, an appreciation for the other's perspective, and an unselfish focus on doing what is best for the customer.

The following Relationship Health Assessment (RHA) can be used to evaluate the overall health of collegial relationships.

Relationship Health Assessment (RHA)

Directions: Think of a colleague with whom you would like to foster a better working relationship, and then score the extent to which you agree or disagree with each statement.

Strongly Disagree (0 points)
Disagree (1 point)
Neutral (2 points)
Agree (3 points)
Strongly Agree (4 points)

_____ I can tell the other person what I am thinking and feeling without fear of judgment.

_____ When we disagree, we have a calm, direct, and respectful conversation.

_____ I feel listened to and understood.

_____ There is a sense of mutual trust between us.

_____ We provide feedback to one another in a constructive and supportive manner.

_____ I would characterize our relationship as collaborative.

_____ We have mutual respect for one another.

_____ I can rely on the other person to keep his/her word.

_____ I believe that the other person has my best interests at heart.

_____ I enjoy working with this person.

_____ **Total Score**

Score Interpretation

0–10   The relationship is broken. There have likely been several negative interactions over time that led to a profound loss of mutual trust and respect. Both people actively avoid one another and communicate only when necessary. Any appearance of collaboration is superficial. In a direct report and manager relationship, the direct report may feel compelled to outwardly feign a certain degree of respect. The prospect of repairing such a relationship is extremely low and an investment in doing so probably not worthwhile. Realistically, it would be best if one person were to move to a new role or exit the organization.

11–20   The relationship is dysfunctional. Differences of opinion likely lead to conflict or disengagement. Pragmatically, it would be best if there were little need for collaboration. Improving the health of the relationship would likely require an intervention by a strong manager or outside facilitator, as well as a sincere commitment from both parties. (In my experience, if the manager had the skill and willingness to address conflict between team members, he would have already done so.) With effort, some level of mutual respect and an openness to each other's viewpoints is achievable. Hopefully, significant confrontations will be avoided. Maintenance and oversight of the relationship is strongly recommended; otherwise, gains will likely be short-lived.

21–30   These relationships are common in the workplace. When differences of opinion arise, both people are likely to feel strongly about their position but are willing to listen to the other's point of view. They are cordial, professional, and respectful toward one another. The success of the relationship is shared equally, and neither maligns the other or intentionally causes conflict. Communication is most often open and forthright, though there are times when each may withhold information that could make them or their point(s) vulnerable. This relationship is on solid footing and could become even more collaborative if both parties were interested and committed to doing so.

31–40 This is a very healthy and productive relationship. There is mutual support, trust, respect, and a strong sense of security and safety. Each person takes full responsibility for the health of the relationship and conversations are straightforward and collaborative. Each person takes the initiative to ask questions to ensure full understanding of the other's views and ideas. They naturally collaborate and focus on what is in the best interest of clients and the organization. Each person willingly admits his or her own mistakes and acknowledges the other's contributions. There is no sense of win or lose in the relationship. When disagreements do occur, they are dealt with respectfully and resolved quickly.

(For additional RHA worksheets and information regarding rights of usage, email me at: Paul@PaulMarciano.com.)

As you look at the results, is the relationship where you want or expect it to be? If not, what specific areas seem most problematic? Try to identify specific interactions that have caused a rift in the relationship. For example, you may have discovered that your coworker spoke poorly about you behind your back, which led to a decreased level of trust. Or, perhaps, whenever you offered a suggestion, she dismissed it without consideration. Have you tried to address the issue? Might this person be open to having a conversation, or would a "Let's talk about it" be met with "Let's not"? If the relationship is not as collegial as you would like, my strong recommendation is that you do something about it, starting with initiating an honest and authentic conversation. If you apply what you have learned in this book, there is almost no chance that a relationship will deteriorate and every chance that it will improve.

Step 2: Be Honest with Yourself

The starting point for restoring any relationship is a sincere willingness to do so. You need to have a frank conversation with yourself and decide how much work you are willing to put into the endeavor. Is there a driving motivation behind your desire to restore your relationship? Do you sincerely want to see things improve, or is your boss pushing you to work more collaboratively? Do you think your colleague is even interested in improving the relationship, or will your effort just be a waste of energy? What is the downside to leaving things as they are? What is the upside to improving the situation? If you authentically want to restore the relationship with your colleague, move to the next step.

Step 3: Initiate the Conversation

Assuming that you are willing to invest the time and energy in restoring the relationship, you will need to begin with a genuine conversation. Be straight, honest, and clear. For example, you might say something like, "Grace, I don't feel as though our relationship has been the same since we argued about whose fault it was that the project did not launch on time. I apologize for how I acted and want to know how I can make things right. Would you be open to having a conversation about getting our relationship back on track?" Hopefully, she will say yes and you can set a time to speak. If she says no, let her know that you respect her decision and are committed to fostering a respectful, collaborative working relationship. If possible, on your own, start by "cleaning up" what you believe may have been the originating incident. In this case, this may involve going to your boss or the client and accepting responsibility for what occurred.

Step 4: Focus on Trust

If you do find that mutual trust is missing or broken, your priority must be on establishing or restoring it. Trust takes time to develop, and once broken, it is incredibly difficult to restore. Whether trust has been broken for one party or both, this issue must be addressed head-on. One way is to tackle it directly and authentically: "Li, I would very much like to build a more collegial relationship with you, and I think it would result in greater productivity. In order to be as collaborative as possible, we obviously have to trust one another, and I don't think that is currently the case. Are you open to having a conversation about our relationship and improving it?" Simply being forthright will have a positive impact on trust.

As always, a good idea is to look in the mirror and ask yourself the following questions:

- ► Can my colleagues trust that I have their back?

- ► Do people know that I will stand up for them if others start speaking poorly about them?

- ► Can people trust that if I have concerns I will speak directly *to* them and not *about* them?

- ► Can I be trusted to be discreet?

- ► Can I be trusted not to take advantage of a colleague or to try to gain an advantage at his expense?

- ► Can others trust that I will be transparent and not withhold information?

➤ Can others trust that I will put the needs of the team or organization above my own?

➤ Can people trust me to keep my word?

Can you answer in the affirmative to all or most of these? If you find yourself answering "No" or "I don't know," start engaging in behaviors today that will increase trust in those areas.

Step 5: Hone Your Interpersonal Skills

When it comes to building collaborative relationships, the first stop is you. What have you done to improve your interpersonal skills? Reading this book certainly counts! But you can also take initiative by doing any of the following:

➤ Perusing other self-development books, articles, or blogs

➤ Watching TED or TEDx Talks

➤ Completing online training classes

➤ Taking in-person workshops related to communication, collaboration, teamwork, or emotional intelligence

➤ Asking for coaching or mentoring at work

➤ Requesting advice and feedback from colleagues and/or friends

Please note that most resources are free or very inexpensive, so cost cannot be your excuse. Also, you do not have to invest a tremendous amount of time to learn and practice these skills. If you are reading this book, you are likely to engage in other continuous learning opportunities as well. The challenge always seems to be reaching those who could benefit the most from "soft skills" training but have little interest in self-development. We tend to spend a lot more time at work improving processes and procedures than we do improving ourselves. In fact, the vast majority of people spend no time working on themselves from an interpersonal skills standpoint. I find that in large part this is due to people's blind spots around how their behavior adversely impacts others.

If you find yourself repeatedly getting into conflicts or arguments with others, it is likely not a coincidence. An excuse I have heard countless times is that the other person is the problem or the one being difficult. Of course, hardly anyone raises a hand when you ask who has poor communication or interpersonal skills. In addition to honest introspection, feedback from colleagues is a valuable resource. If your company offers a 360-degree assessment, you should go through the process, especially if you manage people. Always approach such an assessment in the spirit of curiosity and continuous improvement; you should be disappointed if you do not receive any constructive feedback because it may suggest that your colleagues are not invested in your development or fearful of retribution. (If you are interested in such an assessment and your company does not offer one, please email me at: Paul@PaulMarciano.com.)

Step 6: Develop Your Emotional Intelligence

People with a high EQ tend to be naturally skilled when it comes to building and maintaining healthy relationships. Such individuals are aware of their own and others' emotional states. They understand how their behavior impacts others, can actively manage their feelings and reactions, and are effective at navigating relationship dynamics. And yes, empathy plays a key role. Obviously, such individuals are not only good at dealing with conflict but are able to approach situations and conversations in a way that minimizes the likelihood of conflict, or prevents it from occurring altogether. While it is difficult to increase one's EQ and empathy, it is not impossible, given desire, time, and effort. The key to improvement is role-playing different interpersonal scenarios to practice and test how best to respond to others about sensitive issues.

One of my most frustrating coaching assignments was with Albert, an individual with extremely low EQ and no interest in improving. He was a high-level executive hired to turn things around in the sales department of a multinational organization. However, after almost a year in the position, nothing had turned around other than his boss's patience. A 360-degree assessment revealed that his department's lack of progress was due primarily to his poor leadership skills and inability to build relationships with his team members. In fact, after all those months, he still had not met one-on-one with his 10 direct reports. While he had perfectly good social skills, he was devoid of empathy and had no emotional awareness. He also had no interest in learning about others but would happily share in great detail what was going on in his world.

During my second meeting with Albert, his administrative assistant knocked on the door to inform him that there had been a change in his schedule. After she left, I asked, out of curiosity, how much he knew about her personally. He could not think of one thing. I pushed, "Do you know if she has children? Is she married? Does she have any hobbies outside of work?" He had no idea. In the 10 minutes I spoke with her before meeting with Albert, I learned that Darlene and her husband had just celebrated their twentieth wedding anniversary, the name of their favorite restaurant, were the proud parents of twin boys in high school, and had just gotten a golden retriever puppy named Chamois (her picture was adorable). Although Albert made some minor efforts to change, he was simply too egocentric and narcissistic to ever sincerely be interested in others and thus engender the loyalty of his people. He was ultimately terminated.

Human interactions can get messy, especially when emotions run high, and you need to be prepared to respond when curveballs come your way. For example, how would you respond if you said, "I am sorry to hear that you did not get the promotion" and your colleague replied, "No, you're not!" When people first seek to demonstrate empathy and interest in the interpersonal lives of their team members, they may come across as awkward, inauthentic, and insincere; thus, it is best to make incremental changes in behavior to allow yourself to feel more comfortable and to give others time to adjust to the new and improved you.

My client Zack was a young, driven executive with tremendous potential. While the overall feedback from his 360-assessment was extremely positive, his lack of empathy was his Achilles' heel. This was not news to him, as his highly emotionally intelligent wife, Michelle, had given him the same feedback for years. Unlike Albert, Zack was committed to improving his EQ. Importantly, he was already able to recognize situations that required an empathetic response—he just was not sure what to do. Given Michelle's EQ, I suggested that he try a "What would Michelle do?" strategy. Michelle became his role model and role-playing with her proved extremely effective. Michelle and I were very proud of him!

Another client, Sam, who struggled with EQ, had quite a novel and extremely direct way of dealing with this interpersonal limitation. He would actually tell people, "When it comes to understanding emotions and knowing the right things to say, I'm terrible. My dog and I took an emotional intelligence test and he scored way higher, which was in no way a surprise to me or my wife. It isn't that I don't care; I just don't know how to respond in a way that makes other people feel as though I do. So, if I say something stupid, or don't say anything when I should, I want to save time now and say, 'I'm sorry.' When it comes to emotional issues, I would ask that you be very blunt and explicit."

You do not find many people willing to be this authentic and vulnerable. Being so up front with this issue may go a long way to prevent hurt feelings and conflict situations down the road.

Step 7: Follow Up

It will likely take more than one conversation to fully restore a damaged or dysfunctional relationship. It is important to recognize this and to actively follow up with additional healthy conversations and productive interactions that rebuild trust. Be incredibly transparent and communicate very clearly. Be vulnerable. It is important that you do not give the impression of withholding information or having a hidden agenda. Use the following tips to help win back some lost trust:

▶ In public, show support for others' ideas and only make comments that will be viewed as constructive and helpful, never critical.

▶ Make sure to give credit to the other person; it is always better to shine the light away from you.

▶ Acknowledge and thank the other person when he is being particularly collaborative by saying things like, "I really appreciate your help resolving this."

▶ Admit when you have made mistakes.

▶ Be extremely reliable and consistent.

▶ Use the word "we" a lot.

▶ Set regular check-in times to meet and make sure that the two of you are aligned and any concerns are openly discussed.

▶ When incidents do arise, remind yourself and the other person of your commitment to a mutually respectful and collaborative relationship.

Keep in mind that maintaining high-functioning relationships takes work and fixing them takes even more. Be patient.

Maintaining a Healthy Relationship

Communication is the primary component to maintenance, which means that a healthy relationship is built partially on people talking about issues they may not necessarily want to talk about. When people stop talking and disengage, problems occur. Each party must be willing to speak up during disagreements or when feelings are hurt. Keeping things inside and biting your tongue is a terrible strategy for maintaining a healthy relationship. Continue to practice the many behavioral strategies reviewed in this book, including holding regular check-in conversations.

In sum, the most important behaviors to maintain high-functioning relationships include:

- ► Using open, direct, and straightforward communication

- ► Regularly scheduling times to speak about your working relationship

- ► Listening attentively

- ► Taking an active interest in the other person's work

- ► Being accessible and responsive

- ► Respecting boundaries

- ► Giving constructive feedback

- ► Encouraging and fostering consideration, thoughtfulness, and empathy

- ► Acknowledging and showing your appreciation for others

- ► Keeping commitments; being consistent and reliable

- ► Remaining positive during interactions

- ► Being open to compromise

- ► Being direct when asking your colleague what she needs from you and when telling her what you need

If you want a relationship to remain healthy, you must give it attention. It is a whole lot easier to prevent problems than to fix them.

SUMMARY

I hope that one of the key takeaways for you in this chapter is the importance of being extremely intentional in fostering healthy relationships in your life. Take the initiative to get acquainted with new colleagues, and let them know they can count on your support. When relationships do get fractured, deal with them as quickly and straightforwardly as possible. Do not expect them to heal overnight, but know that they will improve with effort. Work to maintain your relationships every day. Take time to speak about non-work-related issues with genuine curiosity. Always seek to connect with your fellow team members—especially if your relationship occurs primarily over a monitor than in person. EQ is essential to building, restoring, and maintaining healthy relationships. If this is an area of interpersonal weakness for you, make the investment to improve. It will pay dividends in both your professional and personal lives.

UP NEXT

The final chapter will discuss when it is time to move on from a relationship and leave you with critical takeaways.

ON YOUR PLAYING FIELD

1. Choose a colleague with whom you have had little inter-action. Take the initiative to get to know her on a more personal level and see if you can build a sense of connection.
2. How high is your EQ? Are you empathetic and skilled at dealing with interpersonally sensitive issues? If not, identify some educational opportunities and find someone in your life who can serve as a coach in this area.
3. Invite someone with whom you have had a strained rela-tionship to have an open conversation about how you can foster a more productive working relationship. Perhaps, sug-gest that the two of you complete the Relationship Health Assessment and share your results.
4. Review the key behaviors associated with building healthy relationships, and identify three to focus on during your daily interactions with others.

CHAPTER 13

LAST WORD

When it comes to addressing contentious situations, there is no perfect conversation, but hopefully, at this point, you realize that you can foster healthy conversations even in the face of conflict. Furthermore, you can erase the term "difficult conversation" from your vocabulary; the only difficult conversations you need to have are those you label as such. Remember, we tend to call situations hard when we do not feel competent to deal with them effectively. Addressing conflict takes more skill than courage; skill acquisition increases competence, which raises confidence. Obviously, reading a book full of tips, tools, and strategies is great, but you must practice them on your playing field in order to see positive effects. I suggest starting out with small conversations and building up to more significant ones. Get some experience under your belt before tackling weightier issues.

Some people find themselves in the middle of conflict more than others. Like my friend Rich who says, "Trouble finds me." In reality, Rich has a personality that invites trouble like a front door with a welcome sign. While most of us will find ourselves in discord with others from time to time, if you are always on the highlight reel, you are likely not being a responsible team player. I do not know about you, but I get frustrated and even angry at such people for not having the maturity, professionalism, insight, and consideration to take responsibility for their antagonistic comments and behaviors and work to change them. We tend to lose respect for such people and become resentful for the distraction, awkwardness, and tension they cause the rest of the team.

Despite our frustration, most of us bite our tongue or engage in gossip when we see others acting inappropriately or friction stir between team members. Just like the excuses we use to avoid dealing with our own conflict situations, we come up with a list of reasons why we shouldn't say anything when we become aware of others' interpersonal discord: "It's not my place to get involved," "I don't want to get pulled into their disagreement," or "It's not going to make a difference, so why bother?" Now that you have read this book, you have the tools to support team members dealing with conflict. If you have a good relationship with at least one of the people involved, approach him from a place of genuine concern and ask if he would be open to suggestions on how to deal with the situation. Listen with empathy as you try to understand his point of view and then seek to coach him on a more effective approach to the conversation. Share with him some of what you have learned and help him develop a script and role-play. If you know both people, you may offer to facilitate a conversation— there is likely little downside to this effort and much to gain for them and the entire team. As a bonus, you will gain respect for your efforts.

I am not naive. Some relationships simply cannot and should not be salvaged. Resentment has grown too deep, trust too slim, and differences too wide. Most people stay in situations and relationships far longer than they should. I have never heard anyone say, "I wish I'd stayed in that miserable job with that terrible boss for just six more months." And, in almost every case, once people finally make the decision to move on, they experience a tremendous sense of relief. While taking the initiative to confront conflict is empowering, so is deciding that you have given the relationship your best effort and it is no longer healthy for you to remain. Critically, when you decide that it is time to go, go. Make sure to do so in a respectful and professional manner. Leave any resentment behind. In the words of Malachy McCourt, "Resentment is like drinking poison and expecting the other person to die." Use the tools and strategies in this book to help you foster healthy, supportive relationships, but when those simply are no longer possible, I encourage you to move on.

As I wrote this final chapter, I thought to myself, "Paul, if you could only choose a dozen key tips to share, what would they be?" I suggest that you answer this question for yourself and write them down so you can readily refer to them. Here are mine:

Dr. Paul's Top 12 Tips

1. Take 100 percent ownership in making your relationships work.

2. Maintain a positive attitude; if you do not think that a conversation will go well, it will not.

3. Never again label a conversation as difficult unless you want it to be so.

4. Identify and challenge your biases.

5. When you present your views, remember that they are as unique as your thumbprint, and no more right or wrong than anyone else's.

6. Choose your words carefully; you cannot take them back.

7. When you feel triggered and your blood pressure starts to rise, breathe and take a time-out.

8. Stop making other people wrong so you can be right.

9. Listen with intense curiosity.

10. Demonstrate empathy.

11. Admit when you are wrong.

12. When you screw up, apologize.

SUMMARY

I hope this book has empowered you to have healthy conversations with anyone about anything. Put your learnings into action, and make a difference for yourself and those around you. Lean into the skills and strategies in these pages, and shed any lingering apprehension. Choose to deal directly and confidently with conflict rather than avoid it. And, the next time you find yourself in a situation that needs to be addressed, simply say, "Let's talk about it."

UP NEXT

In the appendices you will find answers to commonly asked questions (Appendix A) and scripts that will guide you through resolving your own interpersonal conflicts (Appendix B). Appendix C provides you with best practices for holding videoconferences to help these meetings go as collaboratively and productively as possible. As a "thank you" for having purchased this book, please contact me at Paul@PaulMarciano.com for a complimentary consultation to help you deal with your own difficult conversation.

ON YOUR PLAYING FIELD

1. What was your main fear about approaching difficult conversations before reading this book? What would you say to yourself now, after finishing it?
2. Make your own list of top takeaways and share them with a colleague.
3. After reading Appendix B, try writing your own script for a personal interaction.
4. Are there any conversations for which you still feel unprepared? Take a minute and think about why. What tips and strategies have you learned that you can apply to the situation?

QUESTION AND ANSWER

n conducting research for this book, I invited people to respond to the following question: "Imagine you have the opportunity to ask the world's leading expert in interpersonal communication for advice on how to approach a difficult conversation. What would you ask?"

Here are some of what I view as the most critical questions and my answers to them:

1. **How do I make sure the person does not feel attacked and become defensive?**

   Focus on using "I"—for example, "I am feeling out of the communication loop" versus "Why aren't you keeping me informed?" Point your finger at yourself: "I'm sorry, but I am confused and would appreciate clarification," as opposed to "You must be confused." Use empathy and validate feelings: "I am sorry you are feeling that way, and I probably would be as well," instead of "There is no reason to get upset over such a minor issue." In general, use language that makes you and not the other person vulnerable.

2. **How do I speak in a way that increases the chance of the other person really hearing me?**

Begin by showing your commitment to understanding what the other person is saying. Use body language that depicts engagement, questions that show interest, and paraphrasing to demonstrate understanding. Your best chance of being heard happens after the other person feels heard. When you seek to present your views, use language and examples that will resonate with and make sense to your listener. For example, if you are a salesperson talking to a lawyer, do so from the perspective of wanting to protect the company and not just making sales numbers. Speak into the other person's listening.

3. **I keep having the same conversation over and over again. The other person says he is going to change, but he always goes back to his old ways. Is there anything I can do?**

The key to this question lies in the words "goes back," which implies that a change actually took place; you just didn't do a very good job reinforcing it. Behaviors that change quickly tend to change back quickly if not reinforced. Although you have likely done so before, you should always check to make sure that the other person fully understood the request and why it was important. Also, make sure that the person has the resources needed to be successful and did not run into any stumbling blocks. If you have used the "confused and concerned" approach, yet the problem persists, be straight: "I feel that we have spoken about this issue several times and nothing seems to have changed. Am I wrong about that?" Assuming that you get at least half-hearted agreement, proceed with, "Is there anything you would like to share regarding why we are back to where we started?" You might also query his understanding of the importance of the task and the implications for not following through as discussed. I find that the primary reasons people do not follow through include: they do not understand what is being asked of them, do not understand why it is important, or do not have the resources and/or skills to be successful. If you are the person's manager and there is still no sustained change after these conversations, then you should formally write him up and document what further actions will ensue if expectations are not met. Do not make empty threats. If you are dealing with a peer, you may have to escalate the issue to your boss. Last but not least, consider that it may be you who needs to do some changing!

4. How do I stop being nervous when approaching such a conversation?

Remember, being nervous primarily comes from a lack of confidence, the antidote to which is gaining skills and experience, and, thus, a sense of competence. Plan for the conversation, envision it, and practice it. Just like giving a talk, the more you practice, the less nervous you will be. Of course, a big contributor to your being nervous is that you say you are. You might also put the situation into perspective by comparing it to other conversations you have had throughout your life that were even more "difficult" but that you managed to work your way through. If it makes you feel better, the other person is probably equally or even more nervous than you!

5. How do I manage what I think will be an emotional or hurt response (the person will be hurt again by me bringing it up, but will also be hurt if I don't acknowledge the past)?

Be honest and acknowledge that the other person might find what you say hurtful but that is not at all your intention. In fact, you feel strongly that if you do not discuss the issue, the situation may well become worse for him. You might say something like, "Toby, I want to share some feedback with you. I worry that it will come across as hurtful, and I apologize for that. However, if we ignore discussing this issue or beat around the bush, I fear that the situation will become more difficult to deal with later." Whenever you are addressing a highly sensitive issue, remember that *how* you say something is just as important as what you say. If you always come from a place of authentically caring about the other person, whatever you say will sound more supportive than critical.

6. **What is the best way to ask someone to resign?**

Realize that giving someone the option to resign rather than be fired is often of considerable benefit to that person because it provides him with the opportunity to leave gracefully under what appears (at least on his résumé) to be his discretion. As always, be direct: "Trevor, it has come to the point where we need to part ways. I have spoken with human resources, and you are being given the option to resign. I will need your answer by the end of the week." Do not engage in any conversation unrelated to this question, and do not be apologetic. The situation should be of absolutely no surprise to the individual because he has received ongoing performance feedback that has been well documented. If this is not the case, you have failed to do your job as a manager. I recommend not saying that you will do whatever you can to help him secure another job because it is largely an empty promise and makes no sense. If you are transitioning this person out of your organization, why would you be advocating for him?

7. **What is the best way to tell someone that she is being let go due to an organization restructuring?**

With great compassion and candor. "There is no easy way to say this, Tania, but as a result of the reorganization, we will be eliminating your position. I am truly sorry." Have human resources ready to offer whatever support they can. Be ready to handle any reaction from crying to yelling with calmness and kindness. Assuming she is a good employee, it would be considerate of you to have already reached out to your personal contacts who may be interested in interviewing her. And during the period she is still employed, be flexible with her schedule to allow her time for interviews. Also, if possible, allow her to have a say in how the announcement of her departure is made. She might, for example, want to tell her closest colleagues first.

8. **How do you determine if additional people (human resources, boss, etc.) should be present for a critical conversation?**

It depends. Having said that, here are some situations in which having another person present may be prudent. If the goal of the conversation is to provide highly critical feedback or reprimand the individual, I would ask a human resources representative to attend and take notes on the meeting. If you are dealing with an individual that you believe will make false claims or allegations regarding the conversation, you will want someone else present and you need to make sure to fully document the interaction. If you are faced with a he-said-she-said situation, bring both people together after speaking with each individually.

9. **My boss is always being critical of my work, and I'm tired of it. How do I just tell him to lay off?**

Try something such as the following: "Luis, I am committed to doing my job to the best of my ability. It seems that recently you have been extremely critical of my work and unhappy with my performance. Am I wrong?" Whatever flavor of yes or no you get, you will want to continue the conversation. Ask him to confirm his specific expectations and the criteria by which your performance will be evaluated. Make sure you are on the same page regarding how tasks are prioritized. Request that you regularly have one-on-one meetings to review your performance and that he immediately bring it to your attention when you are not meeting expectations. I would also ask that he let you know when you are exceeding them.

10. **How do I create the sense of an open and safe environment so people feel as though they can come to me and have difficult conversations?**

    Creating an environment in which people feel they can share openly without fear of being criticized or otherwise adversely impacted is critical. This requires a trusting relationship that comes from showing you have the other person's best interests at heart, always keeping your word, and having a history of authentic and straightforward conversations. In terms of starting the conversation, you might try, "I think we should discuss what happened. I know that it is a very sensitive issue, and I want to assure you that what we discuss will remain between us." Of course, if you have not kept your word in the past, this option is off the table. Under certain circumstances, the other person may feel a greater sense of security and comfort if someone else is in the room. Another tactic that can be helpful is to agree that notes either are or aren't taken; if notes are taken, the other person may find it comforting that there is a record of the conversation, and if they are not taken, you can agree that the conversation is "off the record." I would ask for her preference. Also, make such conversations collaborative in nature and demonstrate a level of vulnerability and humility: "I really appreciate your willingness to share your concerns with me. I honestly don't know how to best address this situation and would appreciate trying to figure it out together."

11. **I was fortunate to get an internal promotion, and now I am the boss of someone with whom I had a good peer relationship. I feel that he is angry about not getting the promotion, and I think he believes he should have gotten it. It is really awkward, and I don't feel that I can ask him to do anything. Help!**

    This is unquestionably one of the most challenging situations. Just be candid. "Elias, I know that you were hoping to get the job, and I can imagine that you are very disappointed, maybe even angry. It is my hope that we will continue to have a good collaborative relationship. If you are still interested in advancing, let's work together to sharpen your skills so you are in the best position possible when another opportunity presents itself." Never take on the I'm-your-boss mindset. Instead, consider giving this person a great deal of autonomy. Since you have an established relationship, you may be in an informed position to give the person some additional responsibilities or opportunities that you know he would find desirable. For example, you might know that he really wanted to receive specific training, and you can make that available. If it becomes clear that the person has a difficult time getting over his disappointment, you might have a sincere conversation about helping him find another role in the organization. Have empathy for him, and imagine if the decision had gone the other way.

12. **I tend to sugarcoat or try to protect people's feelings, and then the person doesn't get the weight of what I'm saying. How can I get comfortable just saying the thing that needs to be said without feeling bad myself?**

This is a common challenge for most people. Begin by asking yourself, "Would I want someone to sugarcoat the feedback to me?" Probably not. Say what you have to say, but have it come from a place of genuinely caring about the other person. It is a disservice to give someone a watered-down message, and she may well end up upset with you in the long run for not being more direct. Personally, I avoid the "sandwich" approach—positive feedback, criticism, positive feedback—for the very reason that the core message becomes diluted. I prefer to stay focused on getting the primary point across. Of course, one thing that will make you more comfortable going into such conversations is the mindset that you are offering constructive feedback that is important to that individual's growth and development.

13. **What is the single most important element in making a difficult conversation effective?**

Maintaining a collaborative mindset. I say this because doing so will lead you to engage in all kinds of key behaviors, such as actively listening to the other person and trying to understand her point of view, seeking compromise, not making the other person wrong, and respecting the other person as a colleague. Any conversation that you enter with the mindset of it being confrontational will lead to counterproductive thoughts and behaviors.

14. **How do you approach a difficult conversation so that it doesn't come across as a personal attack, but rather an attempt to fix a problem and reach the same goal?**

Start by getting full agreement on the goal. For example, "I want to make sure that we are on the same page. The purpose of our conversation is to resolve the billing error with the client." You might then say, "As I see it, there was some miscommunication around expectations, and we both probably should have been more careful in checking things over. I am not interested in finger-pointing or placing blame. That doesn't matter to our client. We just need to concern ourselves with fixing the problem." If appropriate, you might also say, "I realize that I have been trying to place the blame for this on you, and that isn't fair. I can imagine that it may have made you feel like I was attacking you, and I apologize for that." In the vast majority of cases you will get some version of, "Thank you. I appreciate you saying so," at which point, you both can focus your energy on the task at hand.

15. **What's the biggest mistake people make when starting a conversation that's likely to be uncomfortable or perceived as confrontational?**

Using language that is accusatory or denigrating and puts the other person on the defensive—for example, "I can't believe *you* did this," "What were *you* thinking," or "*You* got this all wrong." And, of course, starting with the mindset that it will be uncomfortable and confrontational will lead to verbal exchanges that increase the likelihood of each person becoming defensive and/or aggressive in order to prove themselves right and the other person wrong. Or it may be the case that one or both people may be so conflict-averse that the conversation never really gets off the ground and the core issue is never fully addressed out of fear of escalation. Keep your focus on creating and maintaining a healthy conversation that results in a positive outcome for both you and the other person.

16. I delivered critical feedback to an employee, and now he is totally demotivated. What do I do?

Sounds like you screwed up by being "critical" rather than "constructive." As always, be straight. "Ludwig, I have noticed that you have been less engaged since our conversation, and I apologize if my feedback came across as harsh. I shared what I did because I want you to be successful. Was there anything in particular that I said that you found upsetting?" If sincere, apologize. For example, "I am sorry that my comments came across as overly critical. It was not my intention. I respect you and believe that I owe it to you to be honest." Keep coming back to the theme that your goal in giving the feedback was to be constructive and was in no way meant to demoralize him. You may want to ask if there is anything that you can do to help the other person get fully back in the game. Also, make sure to set the person up for success with the next assignment and offer authentic praise for a job well done.

17. Whenever I try to deliver critical feedback, the other person criticizes me for things not going well.

Beyond remaining extremely open to the other person's feedback and perspective, I would actually invite it, "Ibby, I want to discuss what is going on in terms of getting the reports back later than we'd agreed. Let me start by asking your view of the situation." Expect the person to blame you. Remain calm and avoid acting defensively; ask questions and paraphrase to show you are committed to understanding her perspective. Assume responsibility for your part: "You are right. I should have made sure that you had gotten those numbers sooner. I believe we both had a role to play. My goal in discussing the situation is to make sure we are clear regarding responsibilities and expectations going forward." Do not let the other person's criticism dissuade you from holding her accountable.

18. **How do you deal with a colleague who lies, cheats, and steals? People who are just fundamentally bad?**

To the extent it is possible, don't. Have as little interaction as possible, and document any inappropriate behavior. Report more egregious acts to your manager and human resources. Communicate as much as possible over email so that you have a record of conversations. As much as you may be tempted, avoid bad-mouthing or gossiping about the person. You do not want to give him any fodder to use against you. At the same time, protect yourself by building alliances with other team members who can have your back.

19. **How do you approach conversations with people who don't think they are part of the problem when the fact is they are at the center of it?**

You need to start by getting buy-in from the person that there is, in fact, a problem. However, I would replace the word "problem" with "issue," "concern," or "challenge," as people are more likely to admit to playing a role in such situations rather than being responsible for a problem. Using this alternate language also makes addressing the situation less daunting. Recognize that underlying this question is the assumption that the person must be aware of and understand her role in the "problem" in order to make changes in behavior to alleviate it. I would challenge this hypothesis. It is not necessary to convince people that they are part of the problem for them to be part of the solution. In fact, people may be more willing to offer assistance if they do not feel blamed. Your goal should be to make the other person feel empowered to take actions that will make a real difference in improving the situation. With all this in mind, start with a very open-ended question, such as, "What is your take on the client's concerns?" Then probe a little further: "What are your thoughts on how to get things back on track?" You might then ask a question such as, "At this point, what do you suggest we should each be doing?" In general, just focus on getting agreement that something needs to be done differently and then have a problem-solving conversation around it.

20. **What do I do if in the middle of the conversation the other person starts to get very emotional, for example, cries or yells or even walks out?**

If the person walks away, that is fine. Let her. Wait for her to follow up within the next 24 hours, and if she does not, reach out to her. Regarding crying, if you get the impression that the person will be able to compose herself quickly, just remain present and calm. If there is a tissue box nearby, offer it. If the person is extremely emotional, suggest that she take whatever time she needs to compose herself. In terms of yelling, request that the other person lower her voice. If she does not, say that she can reach out once she has calmed down, and then walk away or end the video call. Obviously, all these responses are tempered by your relationship history with this individual. For example, if it is a good friend who starts becoming emotional, you would likely offer comfort.

21. **I just found out that a new hire with less experience is making more than I am. I am extremely angry and want to approach my boss, but if I say what I really want to, I don't think it is going to go well. How should I approach the conversation so that it is constructive and not destructive?**

This is a lousy and difficult situation to address. I would probably *not* say anything that acknowledges that you are aware of the other person's compensation. I suggest approaching the situation by researching what someone in the position with your credentials and experience is paid. In other words, find out your market value. If your salary is low, ask to meet with your manager to discuss the issue and ask for a raise. As my friend Jeannie says, "You don't get what you don't ask for." Obviously, such a conversation is more natural within the context of a performance review, so if you have one coming up, hold off until then. If you do not get an increase, try to negotiate a bonus or raise based on reaching certain performance goals. Another classic way to go is simply to get yourself another job offer, and if you really want to stay with your current company, ask that they at least match it.

22. **I have an employee who is very enthusiastic and is always coming up with ideas and suggestions that, unfortunately, really aren't very helpful. I am afraid that if I keep shooting down his ideas he will become demotivated.**

Before you start focusing on why your employee's ideas won't work, make absolutely certain that you are not being closed-minded. Personally, I am a very in-the-box thinker and have found myself dismissing ideas that I view as "out there" and impractical. Without question, there have been times in my life when being more receptive to others' creative ideas would have served me well. Once you've checked in and been straight with yourself, try being candid with your employee: "Tip, I love your enthusiasm and admire your out-of-the-box thinking. I sincerely wish that I was able to come up with such novel solutions. I realize that you have come to me with lots of suggestions, and it seems that I keep shooting them down. I worry that I am going to demotivate you, and that is the last thing I want to do. I respect your creativity and want to make sure that the team benefits from it. At the same time, we need to make sure that we can realistically implement your suggestions. Would you agree with me?" Most likely, he would, and you have opened the door to what will be a very fruitful dialogue.

23. I am used to holding meetings in person, and now they are all taking place over video. Especially when it is going to be a difficult conversation, how should I be doing things differently?

Fundamentally, your approach should be the same. Go into the discussion with clear goals and a positive mindset, and use the strategies and tools you've learned to foster a healthy conversation. Begin the meeting with an introductory statement such as, "I would prefer to be speaking in person and look forward to doing so again, hopefully, in the not-too-distant future." Make sure to attend to any nonverbal cues that may suggest the other person's desire to speak. Obviously, how you end the conversation will be different. In person you would likely shake hands (or bump elbows) and walk out of the conference room together; your separation would be slower and include small talk, as compared to the curt ending of the click of a mouse. Be prepared with a simple, thoughtful, and clear closing, such as, "Yin, I appreciate having this conversation and look forward to following up. I hope you have a good rest of the day." Depending on your relationship and how the conversation went, you might choose to end on a more personal note, "Please give my best to John, and I hope Lina's college applications are going well."

Perhaps most importantly, recognize that people may be experiencing many stressors while working at home. So, if the conversation you plan on having concerns a performance issue, consider giving that person some latitude and have empathy for her circumstances. An initial conversation to fully understand the challenges the person may be facing and discuss how you might support her would be appropriate.

SCENARIOS AND SCRIPTS

The following scripts are based on real-world scenarios. It is important to recognize that no script is one-size-fits-all. The most effective way to deal with a given situation depends on a number of factors such as the context, your relationship with the individual, your personality and that of the other person, the history of the issue, and the significance of the outcome. Each situation is unique, and there is no singularly right way to hold a critical conversation—other than to focus on it being a healthy one. Use the tools and strategies you have learned in this book, as well as your own experience and common sense, to help guide and steer the dialogue.

Note: To protect privacy, names have been changed. Contributors are included in the Acknowledgments.

Scenario #1

Anna is a mental health practitioner and has been working at a residential treatment facility for the past six months. During this time, there have been several instances in which she felt disrespected by her boss, Sandra, and considered quitting. However, she likes her job and coworkers and would prefer to stay if she were treated better. She decides to talk to Sandra about her concerns.

> **Anna:** "Thank you for meeting with me. I wanted to speak with you about some instances in which I have not felt as though you respected my clinical judgment and decisions."
>
> **Sandra:** "I don't understand. I respect you and your skills very much!"
>
> **Anna:** "You do? It is often difficult to see that. I feel as though you don't appreciate my experience and opinions. For example, during our recent team case review meeting, I said that I would be performing a certain clinical test on Mr. Smith, and without any discussion you ordered me to conduct a different one. I felt embarrassed and disrespected in front of my colleagues."
>
> **Sandra:** "I recommended that test because I felt it would close out the case more quickly."
>
> **Anna:** "Oh, I didn't know that. However, I was the clinician working with Mr. Smith, and in my opinion the test I selected would have given us better clinical data. I would have at least appreciated the opportunity to discuss the matter. I also felt disrespected when I was asked to attend a meeting on very short notice and was not able to rearrange my schedule to do so. Then, apparently, your boss commented that my absence was unacceptable."
>
> **Sandra:** "Wow, I am really sorry to hear about all this and only wish I had been aware of these instances sooner. I do appreciate your coming to me. We talk about the importance of showing respect to our clients, but apparently, in these instances we don't seem to have done that with you. This could reflect a systemic problem with our culture. You are a critical part of the team, and I don't want to lose you. Please tell me what you are thinking."
>
> **Anna:** "I want to work here. And I want to help improve the culture. I think we need to improve communication and to foster a more collaborative atmosphere in which everyone's opinions

and ideas are listened to and valued. Along with increased transparency, autonomy, and decision-making responsibility, people would feel more respected. I know that I would."

Sandra: "Anna, I completely agree and commit to working with you and other staff to improve the culture. Thank you for your willingness to share all of your thoughts and for your dedication to our facility."

Scenario #2

A salesman, Jeff, needs to have a conversation with an important customer who is being unreasonable. He asked that an order be filled a certain way, it was, and now he is claiming that it is not what he asked for. A videoconference call is scheduled.

Jeff: "Good morning, Harnish [many pleasantries]. I wanted to chat with you today regarding the shipment last week under PO number 0621. I understand that you were not happy with the delivery. Could you tell me about the issue?"

Customer: "Yeah, we received a box of parts, and they were bulk packaged. We expected stack packaged parts. We opened the box, and parts were everywhere. The parts are damaged and we cannot use them."

Jeff: "Understood, obviously a frustrating situation. Did you get a chance to send pictures to the plant?"

Customer: "No, we haven't had time."

Jeff: "Harnish, we want to make things right. We need your help to get pictures and document what happened. It is important to understand if the parts were damaged in transit or when they left our facility. When will you be able to get pictures to us?"

Customer: "I will have them emailed over this afternoon. When will I receive replacement parts?"

Jeff: "Harnish, you have been a customer for a long time. We will do what we can to get you back into production. We don't stock those parts; as you know, everything we do is made to order. We also need to understand the disconnect on how we shipped the parts versus how you received them. The drawing specifications on the order indicate that 'parts should be bulk packaged and double bagged.'"

Customer: "One of my people called and left your plant manager a message that we needed these stack packaged. Clearly, you have communication issues going on."

Jeff: "Harnish, you know we have to ship to specification. We cannot change packaging without written approval. This puts my company in a tough spot. It is going to be challenging for us to get parts to you this week. How about we propose working through the damaged pallet, so you can get back into production. If you sort at your facility, we will give you credit for damaged parts."

Customer: "That seems reasonable."

Jeff: "Great. In the meantime, we will need you to update the specification to show stack packaged, and I will work with the plant on a revised quote."

Customer: "I can do that. Thanks."

Scenario #3

William, a new team member and recent MBA graduate, is having difficulty working collaboratively with Jasmine, a team member of 20-plus years, and discusses the situation with his manager, Vania.

William: "Thanks for taking the time to talk today. I'm having a really difficult time working with Jasmine."

Vania: "Tell me what seems to be the issue."

William: "Well, I try to bring new ideas to the team to make us more efficient and to eliminate some of the manual processes, but she cuts me off in meetings and does not appear interested in any of my suggestions."

Vania: "Thank you for coming to me to try to work this out. I appreciate your efforts to improve our processes. There is one thing you may not know that might help you understand how Jasmine is responding. Did you know Jasmine was the person 10 years ago who developed the methodology and processes we are currently using? It may be hard for her to hear that you want to make changes."

William: "I did not know that. I certainly did not mean to insult her. In fact, what she created was really innovative given the technology back then. It is just that by using new computer modeling we could be far more efficient. Do you have any advice on how I can work more collaboratively with her?"

Vania: "Why don't you start by asking Jasmine to tell you about the changes she made and her motivation for doing so. I think you'll find that she too wanted to improve efficiencies. Engage her in a conversation about what she thinks is currently working well and areas in which she feels there may be an opportunity for improvement. She knows the current systems better than anyone and can help you get a full understanding of them before making changes. You may gain her respect and valuable input by demonstrating respect toward her and what she has accomplished. Start by building the relationship before you start trying to build a new system."

William: "Thanks. That is great advice. I imagine that the way I've been acting she probably sees me as arrogant and not respectful. I am going to reach out to Jasmine today and apologize for how I have been coming across."

Vania: "Great! I think she will be very receptive. Let me know how it goes."

Scenario #4

Dana, the newly hired VP of communications, was missing the mark in her new role in the organization. After 90 days in the position, it was apparent that she was driving programs that were not the priorities set by the CEO, Rupen. Her peer, James, was the VP of HR and had befriended Dana. In speaking with Rupen, James knew that he was unhappy with Dana's performance, and James wanted to support her. He reached out and scheduled a video call with her.

James: "Dana, I wanted to check in to see how things are going. Is everything working out as you expected or hoped? Is there anything I can do to help you navigate the politics around here?"

Dana: "Thanks. I think everything is going pretty well. I have built some good relationships here, and I think I've really made an impact in some areas. I made great progress in getting the attention of Senator Smith. We're a major employer, and it's good that he knows who we are and how big we are in the state. I'm excited that after our phone call he agreed to visit the manufacturing facility next month."

James: "Congratulations! Having that connection could prove very useful down the road. How have you been doing with some of the other things that the boss said were priority items? I know that the internal communications program is high on his list."

Dana: "I have done a few things. I scheduled some town hall meetings, and I am working with him on his newsletter. I do wish he was a bit more open-minded to my ideas, though. There are some big opportunities here, and he hired me to make a difference. I could do that if I had more autonomy and resources."

James: "I think it is great that you are thinking big picture. At the same time, Rupen sees the internal communications program as a key reason he brought you in."

Dana: "But I feel that I can contribute much more and have a larger impact within the organization if I get an effective government affairs program off the ground."

James: "I would like to offer you some collegial advice. It's really important to align your agenda with the boss's agenda . . . not the other way around. You've got to deliver on what he says are his priorities. Score points by knocking out his tactical programs. If you do that, he may give you more autonomy to work on other projects."

Dana: "I really appreciate you being straight with me. Between us, I don't feel Rupen has been that clear with me. Or maybe he has and I just haven't wanted to listen. Either way, it is time for me to course-correct. Thanks for having my back."

Scenario #5

Devon, the HR manager, had recently conducted two exit interviews with employees from the IT department headed up by Betto. Both mentioned Betto's management style and treatment of them as reasons for resigning. Specifically, they noted that he would frequently raise his voice and be publicly critical of team members' performance. Based on these interviews, Devon decided to have a 360-degree assessment conducted. The following conversation took place during the debrief.

Devon: "Betto, I have the results of your 360 and want to review them with you. [He hands Betto a copy of the report.] As you can see, there is quite a discrepancy between how you score yourself and how your direct reports score you on items such as 'Is open to feedback and suggestions,' 'Treats others with respect,' 'Provides critical feedback in a constructive manner,' 'Acts with humility,' and 'Fosters teamwork and collaboration.'"

Betto: "Maybe, but my manager and peers scored me higher."

Devon: "That is true. However, even those scores are below your self-evaluation, as you assessed yourself 'strongly agree' on almost every item. It seems that although you may not have seen opportunity for improvement, others do. Discovering these blind spots can be very helpful in terms of putting together a development plan."

Betto: "If you look at my last performance review, you will see that my manager gave me the highest possible scores and maxed out my bonus."

Devon: "The concern is that your employees consistently scored you low on items that are very important to our company regarding being a people manager."

Betto: "I set high standards, hold people accountable, and get results. Is there anything else that matters?"

Devon: "Actually, there is, including growing and developing your people, coaching and mentoring, fostering teamwork, and serving as a role model for our corporate values, to name a few. In contrast, raising your voice and demeaning team members are not acceptable practices here."

Betto: "What are you trying to tell me?"

Devon: "Based on the 360 feedback and conversations I have had with your manager, colleagues, and team members, I have decided to hire an external coach to work with you over the next six months, at which time we will conduct a follow-up 360 to determine whether there have been improvements in your interpersonal and management skills."

Betto: "I don't need a coach to tell me how to manage people."

Devon: "The data would suggest otherwise. I want you to be successful in our culture, but if you are unable or unwilling to change your management style, I'm afraid we will have to part ways."

Betto: "If working with a coach is what I have to do to keep my job, I will."

Devon: "I would ask that you keep an open mind. The coach is excellent, and there is no downside to going through such training—only upside."

Betto: "OK. I will. Maybe she can teach an old dog some new tricks."

Scenario #6

Brian, the chief commercial officer, needed to generate some ideas for repairing relationships between his department and another group that prepared price quotes for customers. He had gotten feedback from his boss that he needed to stop making all the decisions for his people and start engaging them. He scheduled a Microsoft Teams meeting to better understand why relations were deteriorating and to brainstorm some solutions. He asked his colleague Gabriela, who was familiar with the situation, to join the meeting. Afterward, Gabriela and Brian stayed on the call to debrief.

> **Brian:** "What just happened? I take the time to hold a team meeting so I can get input and try to engage people in collaborating on fixing the problem, and all I get are blank stares. I should have just taken care of the situation myself to begin with."
>
> **Gabriela:** "I can tell that things didn't go well in the meeting, and I expect that's not the first time your team has sat silent when you asked for their input."
>
> **Brian:** "Exactly. They never speak up. Never offer any solutions. But they sure do complain and point out what's not working."
>
> **Gabriela:** "Have you thought about what you might be doing or not doing that makes them stay quiet? Anything you may say or do that stops the two-way conversation?"
>
> **Brian:** "What do you mean . . . what is it that I do? I'm the boss, and they should be happy that I ask for their suggestions."
>
> **Gabriela:** "You might be right, but work with me on this. What do you do when an employee suggests something that you don't think will work?"
>
> **Brian:** "I tell them exactly what I am thinking . . . I don't want to waste time chasing a half-baked idea that I know won't get the job done."
>
> **Gabriela:** "It seems that you told your team that this would be a brainstorming session, which most people think of as a

time to share any thoughts they have without judgment. Did you ever stop to think that by reacting so quickly and negatively you are sending the message that you only want suggestions that align with your thinking, and you really aren't open to hearing others? If you really aren't open to hearing your team's ideas, then you should just make decisions on your own. However, you've got some really smart and talented folks, and I would hate for a good idea to pass you by. My suggestion is that you hold a meeting in which all you do is listen and make sure you understand people's suggestions. Don't make any judgments, and see what they come up with."

Brian: "Well, I guess you're right. I do have some great folks, and I do want to hear their ideas. I know that I can be stubborn and 'old school' at times. It will definitely go against my nature, but I will give it a try. Thanks for your support and advice."

Gabriela: "You are welcome. Your team members are going to feel a lot more respected with that approach, and I am sure that you will see more engagement."

Scenario #7

The company president, Yaser, needs to have a discussion with a project manager, Molly, whose department is being ineffective. The company was recently bought by new owners, and though Molly was brought in to improve results and execution, her impact has been disappointing. Despite several discussions, her team is not keeping a critical project on track, and she seems nonchalant about the situation.

Yaser: "Molly, thanks for coming by. I wanted to get an update from you on the project. I know from our last conversation a few weeks ago that your team was not on track to meet either the timeline or budget. I had asked that you keep me posted, but I have not heard back from you."

Molly: "The team is making great progress. We are still uncovering facts and, of course, have run into some challenges, but they all present great learning opportunities and will make our end product even better. By the way, as you probably know, my team volunteered to take over the company picnic this year and are really excited about it."

Yaser: "Molly, I am glad to hear that the picnic planning is going well, but I really need you to focus on getting the project back on track. Perhaps I haven't been as clear as I should: this project is extremely important to the company, and I am counting on you and your team. The perception by upper management is that the project has been floundering for too long. We need to see substantial headway quickly. Is there anything I should know or can help you with, so the project gets back on track?"

Molly: "Actually, I'm glad you asked. I'm going to need to hire two more analysts. My folks are feeling overwhelmed right now, especially with upcoming Microsoft training and vacation schedules. I was looking on LinkedIn the other day and found some potential candidates. Is it OK to ask Julian in HR to set up some interviews?"

Yaser: "Actually, Molly, it isn't. I know you've heard in the department manager meetings that we are losing customers to our competition at a disturbing rate. The project I gave you is critical to figuring out what we need to do with our pricing, marketing, and service fulfillment. If things don't start turning around quickly, we are going to be facing layoffs and budget cuts."

Molly: "Hmm, I guess I didn't realize how serious things were around here. Sounds like sales and customer service really need to start picking up their game."

Yaser: "Molly, everyone is working hard and doing more with less. I have to level with you. Upper management is losing faith in your leadership, and quite frankly, so am I. If you are not able to get the project back on track, we are going to be forced to look at other options. I am requesting that you get me a revised plan ASAP with specific time frames. Going forward, I would like to have one-on-one update meetings every Friday afternoon, so I know exactly where we stand. Please work with HR to reschedule the training. Am I being clear?"

Molly: "Yes. I am sorry that I haven't fully appreciated the situation and urgency of this project. You will have a detailed plan by this Friday. Is there anything else you need from me right now?"

Yaser: "No. I appreciate you getting things moving and look forward to meeting on Friday. Thank you."

Scenario #8

A department manager, Leah, needs to address a new staff member, Mark, who took the initiative to make changes on forms without consulting her.

Leah: "Hello, Mark. I noticed that you made some recent updates and changes to our registration forms."

Mark: "Yes, I saw that there was a lot of information on the forms that we do not utilize, so I worked with IT to remove the additional information. This will streamline our registration process and make it quicker and shorter for participants."

Leah: "Mark, I appreciate the initiative you took, and we always value input on ways to improve efficiencies and processes. However, some of that information we collect is needed by other departments for annual reporting and funding partners. We are required to report on key aspects of participant information, and while we do not utilize that information in our processes, it is important to capture."

Mark: "I had no idea that other departments needed that information. Can we send follow-up surveys or other communications to participants to collect that information?"

Leah: "We have attempted to collect missing information via surveys and other forms of outreach in the past. Unfortunately, these surveys typically receive only about a 20 percent response rate, rendering our data incomplete. If we require the information up front at registration, we can ensure that we are collecting and providing all of the data needed by our organization."

Mark: "I am sorry. I didn't know."

Leah: "I want to encourage you to continue thinking and presenting ways we can improve our processes and the experience for our participants. But next time, let's discuss the ideas and assemble an internal meeting first, so that we can fully understand the impact of the changes to ensure we are all on the same page."

Mark: "Sounds good."

Scenario #9

Two lifelong friends, Sanjay and Peter, founded a start-up together. Happily, the company was successful and grew to 40 employees. Up until that point, they were acting as co-CEOs, which worked well when the company just had a few people, but with 40 employees, it started to become untenable and suboptimal. Sanjay decided to have the difficult conversation with Peter that he wanted just one of them to be CEO so there would be a clearer leadership structure.

Sanjay: "There's something I need to talk to you about regarding the management structure of the company."

Peter: "Oh, really? What's up?"

Sanjay: "I've received feedback from employees that it's not always clear who's making the final decision on certain key strategic issues. While we're normally in sync on 90 percent of issues, when things come up on which we hold differing views, it's challenging for employees to navigate."

Peter: "I see. So what are you proposing?"

Sanjay: "I know for a long time we have essentially been co-CEOs, but now that we have such a large team and different departments, I think only one of us should be CEO. I'd really like to take on that role. And I propose that you be CFO. This way, I can focus on leadership-related responsibilities, while you concentrate on revenue generation. Obviously, we would continue to be partners in making the big strategic decisions for the organization, but in cases on which we differ and a clear decision needs to be made, I'm asking that you entrust me with that for the benefit of the company."

Peter: "OK, this isn't an easy thing. What you are proposing never occurred to me. Let me sleep on it and get back to you."

A few days later:

Peter: "OK, I've had a chance to really reflect on your proposal. At first when you suggested this change, I was taken back. We've been co-CEOs for years, and I think it has worked fine. So my first reaction was 'No way!' But as I reflected on it, I began to understand it from the perspective of the employees and how it might put them in a difficult situation when they get two different answers from us. For their benefit, I will agree to you being the sole CEO, provided that we both commit to being equal partners in making major strategic decisions for the organization."

Sanjay: "Absolutely. I give you my word. Thank you so much. That is one of the most selfless acts I've seen anyone do at any company I've worked at. It reminds me so much of why I knew we would be great business partners to begin with."

Epilogue: The decision to create a sole CEO role turned out to be the right choice as it gave employees much-needed clarity regarding the leadership of the company. Sanjay and Peter continued to make key strategic decisions collaboratively, and together they guided their start-up to a successful acquisition by a publicly traded company. They have remained great friends to this day and have recently begun working together on their next business venture.

Scenario #10

A new female staff member, Lulu, who works as a design consultant, lodged a complaint against a male colleague, Patrick, alleging harassment based on her being a female. Darryl, the HR manager, headed up the investigation, and it was determined that the allegations did not amount to harassment. However, it was also determined that there were behaviors by both parties that were not conducive to creating a positive work environment. It was decided that both should undergo Respect in the Workplace training. The discussion with Patrick went well; however, the conversation with Lulu was more challenging, as she refused to accept any responsibility.

> **Darryl:** "Good morning, Lulu. I wanted to follow up with you this morning on the allegations you made regarding your colleague Patrick. As you were made aware, we conducted an investigation into your concerns, which we have now completed. I want to discuss the findings with you."
>
> **Lulu:** "Great, I am looking forward to hearing what actions will be taken against Patrick."
>
> **Darryl:** "Let me first run down the steps we took. We spoke to you, Patrick, your manager, and several colleagues that are involved with you both on a daily basis. We asked each for very specific instances in which they saw interactions between the two of you. There were some themes that began to emerge from those witness statements."
>
> **Lulu:** "I bet there were. However, since this is a male-dominated environment, I am sure that they are all siding with Patrick."

Darryl: "What we have determined through our investigation is that some of Patrick's communications and interactions with you were insensitive, outdated, and/or patronizing. However, they do not amount to harassment as alleged."

Lulu: (Under her breath) "I knew it."

Darryl: "Nevertheless, we have, and continue to work with Patrick to help him understand how his actions and comments may be negatively perceived by colleagues, clients, and others. In fact, as you mentioned yourself in your original complaint, 'It appears Patrick is making an effort.'"

Lulu: "So what you are saying is that I just need to put up with this. I refuse to, and I refuse to be put in a situation where I have to interact with him."

Darryl: "Lulu, given our findings, Patrick will be participating in Respect in the Workplace training and we expect the same of you."

Lulu: "Listen, I will not accept this, and I refuse to work with Patrick."

Darryl: "Lulu, during our investigation, Patrick also raised concerns about your approach with him, which he, in fact, found overly aggressive and made him uncomfortable. This was a theme that arose with all those we spoke to and was reinforced by a recent vendor call. We were informed that following a tour you took there, you actually called a customer and demanded a calendar posted at a workstation be taken down. Without commenting on the appropriateness, or lack thereof, of the calendar, our company has a policy that requires you to bring such complaints to either human resources or your manager directly. You are not to contact a vendor or customer directly with these sorts of complaints and make demands while acting as a representative of the company."

Lulu: "The calendar was offensive, and I have a right to stand up for myself and not be put in a situation that makes me uncomfortable."

Darryl: "That is exactly right, Lulu. I agree with you, and the company doesn't want you to be put in any uncomfortable position. In the future, you should contact me or anyone in human resources or your manager, and we will determine the best way to reach out to the customer and provide them with the feedback."

Lulu: "So, ultimately, you are saying this is now my fault!"

Darryl: "Lulu, we want you to be comfortable and successful at work. We also have a responsibility to create a positive work environment for others and need to address any concerns that were raised by them in our investigation."

Lulu: "How did I do anything wrong? You are trying to blame the victim. I am a victim."

Darryl: "Lulu, there were several complaints raised about how you speak to people. People were uncomfortable with both your tone and your words. This was displayed in how you responded to Patrick, and that is when it was brought to the attention of his manager. I believe this has previously been mentioned to you. I bring it up only to underscore that we are looking at this situation holistically and want to support the creation of a positive working relationship for you both."

Lulu: "It sounds like you are taking Patrick's side. I didn't do anything wrong."

Darryl: "The company is always trying to improve the environment in which its employees work, and training is a way by which such improvement is achieved. It is company policy that when such accusations arise, both employees must attend training. This training is not disciplinary in nature, nor is it a reprisal of any sort, and we hope you do not feel that way. It is educational in nature, and helps illustrate how an employee sometimes perceives an interaction with a coworker, manager, or other individual in a manner that is inconsistent with the coworker's, manager's, or individual's intention, and inconsistent with how an objective bystander would perceive the interaction."

Lulu: (Aggressively) "I *need* to understand specifics about this training company, their evaluation procedure, and their credentials before I go for any training."

Darryl: "Please rest assured that we have fully vetted the company and their trainers. I want you to understand that you are a valuable member of the team. We will continue to take your concerns seriously and work with you and all employees to ensure our work environment is as healthy and productive as possible. With that in mind, we want to reiterate that some of Patrick's behavior you reference in your correspondence was not (and is not) appropriate, and it was not (and will not be) condoned by the company. If it continues despite our warning, internal coaching, and external training, I ask you to speak to me directly."

Scenario #11

Evander, a shift leader in the sorting department, has been with the company for about a year. During the interview process, it was made clear that corporate values and culture are a priority. Evander is an excellent performer: he is exceptional at picking up new skill sets, his shift is top-tier when it comes to production, and feedback from his team is that they really like working with him. Bob, the plant manager, decided to put together a cross-functional team to deal with departmental silos and asked that Evander participate. Evander came to the first few meetings and gave some good input, but then just stopped showing up. Bob became concerned and asked Evander to come see him.

Bob: "Evander, we have been missing your insight during the cross-functional team meetings. What's going on?"

Evander: "I make production the number one priority for my team and, as you know, the numbers bear that out. My time is better spent out on the floor with my guys."

Bob: "Evander, there is no question that your team is being successful, in fact, exceeding their goals. At the same time, it is important that there is good communication and collaboration across teams. Safety has to come first, and you know we emphasize the importance of our culture—we view it as our secret sauce when it comes to delivering great customer service and fostering employee loyalty and pride."

Evander: "I agree that safety is important, but sometimes I think we take it too far. We have procedures in place that are just overkill. When it comes to culture, I emphasize individual responsibility and hard work. My goal is for my team to outperform the other shifts, and, as you can see, my approach is paying off. Attending these 'feel good' meetings is taking me away from my team and getting the real work done."

Bob: "Evander, that's very concerning, especially since as one of our team leads, you should be serving as a role model for our values. During the interview process it was made clear that we are all committed to living the core values and supporting the company culture."

Evander: "Yes, I remember watching the onboarding video and even signing some document about supporting the values and culture. That is all good, but what you're paying me for is to get a job done, and I am. Look, it isn't like I'm walking around telling people not to act safely or be a jerk to people on other teams. I honestly don't understand what the problem is."

Bob: "Well, that is disheartening, but I appreciate you being straight with me. You are a talented guy and I respect your work ethic, but our company values and culture are nonnegotiable and have to come first. Being that it is Friday, I would ask that you take the weekend and really think about whether this is the right place for you to work."

Evander: "OK, I will do that."

On Monday the discussion continued:

> **Bob:** "Evander, I hope you had a good weekend. I wanted to follow up on our conversation."
>
> **Evander:** "I thought a lot about what we discussed and even talked to some of my guys and another shift supervisor. They shared with me how important the values are to them, and one of the reasons they work here. I can see now that I have underestimated and not fully appreciated the culture. I apologize for that I would like to re-engage with the cross-functional team meetings."
>
> **Bob:** "Evander, I am really pleased that you took the time to speak to team members and appreciate your change in mindset. Of course, you are welcome to come back to the meetings and I look forward to your input."
>
> **Evander:** "Thanks very much."

Scenario #12

Paul was the founder and owner of ColorMe Company, a manufacturer of children's arts and crafts. He hired a college intern, Danny, to help out with the company's technology needs. On Danny's second day, Paul heard him swearing while working on the network. While Paul had certainly done his share of shouting at computers, he was upset because the company was very family-oriented and such language had no place within the culture. The next morning, he asked Danny to come into his office.

> **Paul:** "Danny, we are all excited to have you here, most especially me. I know you are really going to be a great asset to the team. I need to apologize to you because when we first met and I told you about the company, I did not emphasize our values and culture."

Paul handed Danny a copy of the company's foundational document, which included its vision, mission, and guiding philosophical principles and asked him to read it. Afterward, the discussion continued:

> **Paul:** "It is really important that all team members believe in and support what is written on this document. It creates our culture and is what makes our company so special. It was my mistake not to ask you to read it during your first interview. How do you feel about what you read?"
>
> **Danny:** "Wow, I think it is great, and I definitely support what the company stands for. And I know why you wanted to speak with me."
>
> **Paul:** "Why?" (Smiling to himself because he knew Danny "got it.")
>
> **Danny:** "Because I swore yesterday and that goes against ColorMe Company's principles and culture. I promise you that it will never happen again."
>
> **Paul:** "Danny, thank you."

Epilogue: Danny never did swear again, and the internship turned out to be a wonderful experience for him and the organization. And Paul never made the same mistake; he started all interviews by sharing that foundational document and took great pride in seeing all team members bring it to life every day.

BEST PRACTICES FOR VIDEOCONFERENCES

The skills and strategies you have learned in this book apply as much to conversations held over video as they do in person. You prepare, enter with an engaging and collaborative mindset, demonstrate respect, and seek to foster a healthy conversation. At the same time, there are differences that should be considered when having a critical conversation. (While audio-only calls make sense under many circumstances, when it comes to challenging conversations, I strongly encourage doing these "face to face.")

The most significant downsides of having a remote conversation are that you lose the ability to read body language and are more likely to be distracted by the goings-on in your and the other person's environment. If the conversation is likely to become emotional, one or both parties may feel awkward if the discussion can be overheard by family members. In general, individuals with small children at home may enter the conversation in an already frustrated, stressed, and distracted state. And those experiencing video fatigue may be agitated, less engaged, and/or patient. In contrast, others may find themselves more relaxed when having such a conversation in the privacy and comfort of their own home. Remote conversations can also be beneficial to those who deal with social anxiety issues or may feel intimidated when in the physical presence of others with whom they experience conflict.

Virtual meetings can be very helpful when tackling a difficult conversation. Video tends to be a cooler medium, so people are less likely to become emotional during a virtual meeting as compared to an in-person meeting. In certain situations, and with the consent of the other individual(s), it may be helpful to record the meeting, under which circumstances people are more likely to remain calm and reasonable. Another advantage of video meetings is that if one or both people become too upset, the conversation can be quickly ended with the click of a mouse button. Taking a time-out was never easier!

In addition to the skills and strategies you have learned in this book, here are some best practices for videoconferences.

Environment

When working remotely, your goal should be to simulate as professional a work environment as possible. Obviously, having a dedicated home office is ideal, but this is not an option for many people. Regardless of the physical space in which you participate in virtual meetings, here are some general tips:

1. For your own sake and that of others, choose a location that is as free as possible from noise and distractions such as pets, children, and road traffic as possible. If you live with others, let them know when your call will begin and when it has finished, not simply the time at which the meeting is scheduled to end, as it may run long. If you are taking the call in a private room, you may want to lock the door and/or post some version of a "Do not disturb" sign.

2. Keep your background clean, simple, and uncluttered. Some video platforms allow you to blur the background, which I view as ideal.

3. Lighting is critical for others' viewing experience. You do not want to look washed out, cast a shadow, or appear to be broadcasting from a bunker. In general, try using soft direct lighting. (The online videoconference platform Zoom provides detailed suggestions regarding lighting.*)

Physical Appearance

In general, dress and look as you normally would during an in-person meeting. Choose solid and bold-colored shirts, and avoid stripes and patterns that may not reproduce well on-screen. Make sure to be well-groomed. In terms of jewelry or other accessories, keep it simple and choose pieces that will not produce noise when you move your head, hands, or arms. (For tips on wearing makeup, consider the advice of Marnie Goldberg.†)

Technology

The equipment that you use will make a tremendous difference in terms of a quality experience for yourself and others. Equipment that you may consider purchasing includes:

1. Large-screen monitor (Many people find dual monitors very helpful.)

2. High-quality external webcam

3. High-quality and comfortable noise-canceling headset with a microphone

4. Reliable and high-speed Wi-Fi (Check with your Internet provider to determine if upgrading your Internet package

* https://support.zoom.us/hc/en-us/articles/360028862512-Lighting-Concepts.
† https://youtu.be/O7H_XjPtT2o.

makes sense. Depending on signal strength, you may want to purchase a Wi-Fi extender.)

5. White noise machine to drown out distracting sounds

6. Comfortable chair with back support

Pre-meeting Steps for Host

While technology can make virtual meetings go awry for any number of reasons, there are several steps the host can take to increase the chances of a smooth meeting for all participants:

1. In terms of best practices, meeting invites and agendas should be sent at least three days in advance—further out if significant preparation is required of participants.

2. In addition to sending a calendar invite, include the conference link and call-in number in the email, along with the meeting agenda.

3. Should you need to send an updated meeting invite such as a new conference bridge or time, ask all participants to confirm receipt of the updated information. If you do not hear from a participant within four hours of the meeting time, reach out to him directly.

4. Log in 5 to 10 minutes before the scheduled meeting time.

Pre-meeting Steps for Participant

As a meeting participant, there is more to think about than just showing up as you might for an in-person meeting. Be a responsible colleague and adhere to each of the following recommendations:

1. Always have the dial-in phone number nearby as a backup.

2. Close unnecessary programs to reduce distraction and improve computer performance.

3. Have a bottle of water, cough drops, and tissues at arm's length.

4. Turn the ringer off on your phone(s) and mute any incoming email and text message alerts. If you must monitor incoming calls or messages, let others know this at the beginning of the meeting.

5. If possible, log in three to five minutes early. (As a general tip, set an alarm on your phone for five minutes before any meeting, even if you get a pop-up calendar reminder.)

During the Meeting

The following tips are important for all meeting participants to follow and should become standard practices in your organization:

1. Once logged in, check to make sure that your audio and video are working properly. Be certain that your microphone is muted, the speaker icon is turned on, and the volume is appropriately set.

2. When you first log in, you will likely see a video image of yourself. Make sure that the camera is at eye level and about half your torso is squarely in the frame. Most people dislike seeing themselves on video and choose to shut off the self-view. While doing so is fine, you will lose the visual reminder of how you appear to others and may unconsciously make facial expressions that you would prefer not to be viewed by others. I recommend keeping a thumbnail image of yourself on the screen if this is an option. Check to make sure that your background is as you want it and your lighting is adjusted.

3. Ask others to confirm the quality of your video and audio, and request that you be notified of any problems during the meeting. If video is a problem for you or anyone else, turning it off and remaining with audio may be the best option. If you choose to switch to a phone conference, double-check that you have the correct phone number before leaving the video meeting.

4. Keep your microphone muted when not speaking. Remember to unmute yourself when you wish to speak.

5. At the beginning of the meeting, acknowledge and apologize in advance for any potential noises or distractions that are likely to occur.

6. Inform others if you will be taking or looking down at notes or turning your head to view a monitor.

7. Speak as clearly as possible and make sure to keep your hands away from your face to avoid muffling your voice. If you tend to speak quickly, make a concerted effort to slow your cadence. If you tend to speak softly, increase the volume of your voice.

8. Maintain eye contact and use facial expressions that communicate engagement and active listening. In an in-person meeting, attention is focused on the speaker and much less on others. Depending on the video platform and settings, however, in a videoconference you may always be in the picture and readily visible to all participants throughout the meeting. Thus, behaviors such as yawning, bad posture, looking away, texting, fidgeting, emailing, and reading are extremely noticeable. Videoconferences are generally far superior to audio-only meetings or telephone calls as they make participants feel more engaged with one another and greatly reduce the multitasking that commonly occurs during audio-only conferences.

9. If you have to temporarily leave the conference, for example to answer an urgent call or use the restroom, let others know and shut off your video and mute your microphone.

10. In face-to-face meetings, jumping into a conversation is fairly easy. It is not so simple on a conference call (especially audio-only). Many programs allow you to virtually raise your hand. In the absence of this feature, you can literally raise your hand if it can be viewed by the meeting facilitator. In either case, it is best to wait for the facilitator to acknowledge you. If you feel compelled to interject, make sure to use the person's name. For example, "Lexi, excuse me, I just want to ask a question." Remember, it may be difficult for people to read your nonverbal body language, so you may need to be more direct when you wish to join the conversation.

11. Make sure the facilitator has "officially" ended the call before leaving the meeting, and then do make sure to actually leave the meeting.

INDEX

ABOUT THE AUTHOR

Born in the one-bridge town of Three Bridges, NJ, Dr. Marciano earned his doctorate in clinical psychology from Yale University. He has worked in the field of human resources for over 30 years as a consultant, facilitator, trainer, and coach.

He is the foremost authority on employee engagement and respect in the workplace. His bestselling book, *Carrots and Sticks Don't Work: Build a Culture of Employee Engagement with the Principles of RESPECT™*, has received critical acclaim around the world and been translated into several languages. The book provides readers with dozens of specific turnkey strategies that bring about an immediate increase in employee morale and productivity.

Dr. Marciano is passionate about helping individuals and organizations deal with interpersonal conflict, break down interdepartmental silos, and foster collaboration. He is committed to spreading respect in the world and workplace because it is both the right thing to do and because treating people with respect leads to extraordinary business results.

For more information, visit www.PaulMarciano.com.